Training Your Boxer

Joan Hustace Walker

BARRON'S

Important Note

This book tells the reader how to train a Boxer. The author and the publisher consider it important to point out that the advice given in the book is meant primarily for normally developed puppies from a good breeder—that is, dogs of excellent physical health and good character.

Anyone who adopts a fully grown dog should be aware that the animal has already formed its basic impressions of human beings. There are dogs that as a result of bad experiences with humans behave in an unnatural manner or may even bite. Only people that have experience with dogs should take in such an animal.

Even well-behaved and carefully supervised dogs sometimes do damage to someone else's property or cause accidents. It is, therefore, in the owner's interest to be adequately insured against such eventualities, and we strongly urge all dog owners to purchase a liability policy that covers their dog.

All inquiries should be addressed to:
Barron's Educational Series, Inc.
250 Wireless Boulevard
Hauppauge, NY 11788
http://www.barronseduc.com

International Standard Book No. 0-7641-1634-7
Library of Congress Catalog Card No. 00-045541

Library of Congress Cataloging-in-Publication Data
Walker, Joan Hustace, 1962–
    Training your boxer / Joan Hustace Walker.
      p. cm.
    Includes bibliographical references (p.) and index.
    ISBN 0-7641-1634-7 (alk. paper)
    1. Boxer (Dog breed)—Training. I. Title.

SF429.B75 W362   2001
636.73—dc21
                        00-045541
                        CIP

Printed in Hong Kong
9 8 7 6 5 4

About the Author

Joan Hustace Walker has been writing professionally since 1984. She is a member of the Authors Guild, the American Society of Journalists and Authors, the Dog Writers Association of America, the Cat Writers Association, and the Society of Environmental Journalists. Walker writes for both general and technical audiences, specializing in animals, education, aging, and environmental issues. Her other book titles include *The Boxer Handbook, St. Bernards, Old English Sheepdogs,* and *Great Pyrenees.* She has had hundreds of articles published by a variety of magazines, including *Modern Maturity, Family Circle,* and *Dog World,* and was awarded the "Maxwell Award" by the Dog Writers Association of America.

Acknowledgments

This book would not have been possible without the generous help and experience of two extraordinary Boxer trainers, Tracy Hendrickson of Tulsa, Oklahoma and Norbert Zawatzki of Waldsolms, Germany. Also, I am indebted to my friend and translator Rosi Westphal, who always "made it happen" in Germany, and the talented members of the Boxer training club in Wetzlar, Germany. I would be remiss if I left out a special thanks to my talented photographer and brother, Curtis Hustace, who was willing to travel to Germany twice and to locations across the United States in preparation of this book.

Cover Credits

Curtis Hustace: front cover, back cover, inside front cover, inside back cover.

Photo Credits

Tracy Hendrickson: pages 4, 18, 63, 71, 102, 106, and 107; Billy Hustace: pages 11, 95, and 132; Curtis Hustace: all other photos; Mario Mozzati: page 131; Silke Zawatzki: page ix.

Contents

14

Competitive Activities 122

Useful Addresses and Literature 134

Index 139

Foreword

My one wish, as the founder and chairperson of the American Boxer Rescue Association (ABRA) would be for *every* Boxer owner to read this book and train their Boxers. If this could happen, it would make Boxer Rescue obsolete.

Why? Because the main reason Boxers are turned in to shelters is for behavior problems. These abandoned dogs aren't truly "bad," they just haven't received the attention, love, and training that are required to mold *any* Boxer into a respected, civilized canine that the whole family can enjoy.

Tracy Hendrickson and U-ATCH, U-AGI, U-CD, U-CDX, U-CH, AM/CAN/BDA CH Sunchase's Suicide Blonde AM/CAN/BDA CH, CDX, UD, NA, NAJ, OA, OAJ, TT, TDI, CGC, BH, AD, VCC, VCCX, VO, H.I.C. (also known as "Chili").

In this book, Joan Hustace Walker takes readers step by step to help them train their Boxers to become treasured family pets. The author also provides some great insights into what is going on in the Boxer's brain and its many modes of activity. The training methods in the book are specifically tailored with the Boxer in mind, are all positive, and use no force.

And, perhaps best of all, *Training Your Boxer* is written in a style that is lively, interesting, and down-to-earth. The author relates as well to Boxer owners as she does to Boxers!

All Boxers deserve to be loved and enjoyed, and *Training Your Boxer* shows readers how to accomplish this task in a fun-filled way. The additional information on activities and performance events shows the depth at which this breed can compete, and may even spark your interest in a new direction with your Boxer.

However far you decide to take your Boxer in his training, there is just one book you should purchase before or after your Boxer arrives home—*Training Your Boxer*. The Boxer ownership road is full of bumps and curves along the way, but with a good roadmap, you're less likely to get lost.

Tracy Hendrickson
Sunchase Boxers
ABRA, Founder and Chairperson
Owner/trainer: ABC Performance Dog
of the Year/2000

For more than 20 years, I have owned, trained, and bred Boxers. In that time, I also have been deeply interested in all literature that is available on the Boxer. I am delighted with this new book from Joan Hustace Walker. She writes very clearly and in great detail about the Boxer, beginning with the history of the breed and going all the way to the games they play and the training they require.

Training Your Boxer is a great book for a Boxer lover. I met the author in Wetzlar, Germany, a little while ago and I had the opportunity to show her the training we use with German Boxers. I am very honored that some of the information I provided is in this book.

Of course, every time you train a Boxer, you learn something new. We have a saying here in Germany: "All roads lead to Rome—you just need to find the correct one." The road I chose five years ago, always to emphasize the positive, has enabled me to have the success I now have with my Boxers. Operant training also enables me to begin training with Boxers at an early age. The highest principle is never to use force.

With these training principles, I have been able to achieve early results with my two-year-old Boxer, Henry.

I wish all readers great pleasure in reading this interesting book and much success in practicing the methods this book describes.

Norbert Zawatzki and Henry von Nassau Oranien SchH1, SchH2, SchH3 won 3rd place at the ATIBOX World Championships 2000 in Mailand, Italy.

Norbert Zawatzki
Director of Training
Boxer Klub e.v. Sitz Munchen

Preface

The Boxer is a wonderful breed, but with no training his natural instincts and behaviors quickly can create turmoil in the home. The breed's intelligence, enthusiasm, joyfulness, strength, and creativity are all excellent qualities to have in a dog; however, they don't make this energetic working dog easy to train.

Unfortunately, there is no one magic way to train a Boxer. Though many training books tout "the way" to train *all* dogs, this really isn't possible—especially for the Boxer. Why? First of all, because the Boxer as a breed is very different to train than a sporting breed, a hound, or a toy. Secondly, within the Boxer breed itself, you will find a variety of temperaments and abilities, and therefore every Boxer will respond to training differently.

The author enjoys a classic Boxer greeting.

And finally, all trainers and owners are different, from the way they talk and walk, to their mannerisms, athleticism, patience, and even their ability to *read* what their dogs are thinking. This means that every *person* trains dogs a little differently and some methods are easier for them to use than others.

This combination of variables with the breed, the dogs themselves, and the owners means that there is no cookie cutter way to deal with training every single Boxer. If the Boxer owner is given a variety of training tools and strategies to work with that have been proven to be successful with most Boxers, the owner can then determine which training tools work best for him or her.

Training Your Boxer seeks to present Boxer owners with a variety of training strategies, as well as (hopefully) unraveling some of the mysteries involved in training the Boxer. The book takes a look at the psyche of this great canine in order to help explain why he does what he does, and what an owner needs to do to shape these behaviors in a positive way.

I hope you enjoy working your way through this book as much as I have enjoyed writing it. It has been a great pleasure to work with some of the top Boxer trainers in the United States and Germany for tips and successful strategies. Without their generosity and desire to help Boxer owners everywhere, this book would not have been possible.

1 Why Train Your Boxer?

Boxers are great dogs. They're intelligent and athletic, and they love their people. What other breed will routinely do the wriggling, "kidney bean" dance when it greets you at the door? It is no wonder that the Boxer is one of the most popular breeds in United States and Canada, as well as many other areas of the world.

The Boxer, however, needs training in order to become a treasured family pet. Because this breed is an extremely muscular and powerful dog with boundless enthusiasm and energy, it requires early and consistent training. An untrained, unsocialized, full-grown Boxer cannot only wreak havoc at home, but also in the neighborhood.

Boxer rescues relate that all too often a Boxer that has had no training ends up banished to the backyard because her owners can't handle an unbridled, uncontrollable 60-pound (27-kg) whirlwind of solid muscle in the house. Once in the backyard, the Boxer becomes even more miserable because she is separated from the family she loves. Other undesirable habits quickly crop up, such as barking, scratching at the door, digging, and jumping fences.

Usually, it is not too long after she has been cast out to the backyard that the family gives up entirely on the dog and turns her into the shelter or relinquishes her to a Boxer rescue. What is truly sad is that this whole scenario can be avoided if the owner realizes that the Boxer is not an "automatic Lassie," and that training is important and requires commitment and consistency from the owner.

But, you already know that! Just in case you need some additional ammunition to solidify your belief that training is a good thing for both you and your Boxer, read on.

Advantages to a Well-trained Dog

1. **There Is Less Chaos.** As mentioned earlier, if a dog is left to her own ways, she will fall back on the only things she knows—canine behavior or "dog ways." When living with a family, these behaviors are generally unacceptable. Marking the kitchen table, knocking down the kids, and grabbing the roast off the serving plate are all examples of behaviors that are acceptable to dogs, but not to their human families. Simply said, training your Boxer gives you the tools

Boxers can and do make obedient pets.

to develop a well-behaved dog that is eager to please you and abide by your rules—or at least most of them.

2. **Training Identifies and Potentially Reduces Behavior Problems.** If you've done your best to select a Boxer with a wonderful, even temperament, you will most likely never have a problem with aggression or other behavior problems. Since temperament is influenced greatly by the environment, you will want to make sure your puppy grows up in the best environment possible. The easiest way to begin this is to

> **Boxer Byte:** A recent study found that lack of training was the number one reason dogs are relinquished to shelters and pounds. With little or no training, a dog must live the only way she can—by her natural instincts and behaviors. Unfortunately, living by dog rules rather than people rules can quickly create turmoil in the home.

enroll in a puppy kindergarten or preschool class.

If you begin training your Boxer puppy at a very early age, you will be more in tune with your Boxer and will be working with professionals, so, if there are any potential behavior problems, you will be able to identify them early. Animal behaviorists say that the best success rate in correcting behavior problems is if they are recognized and caught early, whereas behaviors that have been allowed to exist for many years are more difficult—if not impossible—to modify.

3. **Training Develops a Well-balanced Boxer, Emotionally and Physically.** The Boxer is truly a "people" dog and thrives on attention. Regular training gives you the quality time she looks forward to and needs. Training sessions also give you an opportunity to exercise with her, and training with gentle, positive, reinforcement-based methods will establish your leadership with her in a gentle, nonconfrontational manner. All of this helps to develop the

Boxer's place in the family as a loyal and trusted pet, and results in a well-balanced dog.

4. **Training Creates a Dog That Is a Joy to Live With.** A dog that will sit while waiting to be served her food, walk without pulling on a leash, and come when she is called (the first time), is a pleasure to live with. Teaching the basic skills of living will develop a Boxer that understands rules of the house and will not try to challenge you or your family.

5. **Training Helps Your Dog Gain Respect from Fearful or Reserved Neighbors.** Though the Boxer continues to have a reputation as a well-tempered dog and not a breed prone toward unprovoked aggression, many people judge the Boxer by looks alone. The short nose, cropped ears, and impressive-looking bite can evoke a wary if not fearful reaction from many people. For this reason, the Boxer owner has an added responsibility to present this breed as a well-trained, congenial dog. If the neighbors are impressed with your dog's impeccable manners while on walks, you're likely to never receive any complaints. However, if she drags you uncontrollably down the street, your neighbors may voice concerns about your "vicious" dog. Totally unfair, yes, but it is best to train her to be an exemplary ambassador for the breed.

6. **Training Lowers Liability (Legal Discussion).** Speaking of vicious dogs also brings us to the legal issues surrounding owning an untrained or unruly dog. Citizens, lawmakers, and insurance agencies are taking an increasingly stern

Boxer Byte: The Boxer's predecessors include the Brabenter Bullenbaisser, which was used centuries ago for hunting boar and, later, for bull baiting. Today, dog fighting is illegal; however, there are reports of Boxers being bred to Pit Bulls to create bigger fighting dogs or to be used as "bait" dogs. Some pet Boxers have their ears closely cropped, similarly to a Pit Bull's ears, making it difficult for some non-dog people to distinguish the Boxer from other breeds. These links could lump the Boxer into some lawmaker's definition of a fighting or bull baiting dog.

Which one? If you can't take time to train, choose the cuddle toy. If you have time to train, however, the Boxer puppy will be an eager and willing learner.

approach toward certain breeds of dogs. Though Boxers are not listed among the top ten injury-causing breeds in insurance claims, there have been discussions to include all breeds bred originally for fighting or bullbaiting in breed-specific laws or bans. There have also been some concerns among Boxer breeders that ignorant humans may try to "make" this breed the vicious dog of the new millennium.

All conjecture aside, the Boxer is a strong, athletic dog with a potentially dangerous bite. A loose Boxer—even if she is the most friendly dog on the face of the earth—is capable of frightening both children and adults with her appearances alone. A Boxer that has some aggressive tendencies is a liability.

Training her will greatly reduce the risk of any accidents occurring, and it may very well be essential in the future if Boxers become targeted by insurers.

7. **Training Creates a Human-dog Bond.** The more you work with your Boxer, the deeper your bond will be with her. Studies have shown, too, that owners who spend time training their dogs and who compete in activities, tend to share their successes with their dogs. They become partners, a team, working toward a common goal. Positive relationships between dogs and their owners are ones in which the owner may reap considerable benefits, such as a longer life, better health, and quicker recovery from surgery, to name a few.

Your Boxer needs to learn to obey everyone, even the littlest family member.

These benefits may be lessened or nullified if your dog is a holy terror. If you spend more time fretting about what she is going to rip up next or which frail family relative is going to be bowled over this time, your untrained Boxer may be causing more complications than you need. The problem is easily solved and the many benefits from the human-animal bond can be gained by simply establishing order and—you guessed it—training your dog.

8. **Training Establishes Children as "Leaders."** If you have children, involving them in the day-to-day training of your Boxer will help her to understand that these little people with the high voices are "masters," too, rather than puppies, playmates, or chew toys. Methods for teaching her to willingly accept commands and handling from your children are included in Chapter 8: Five Commands Every Boxer Should Know (see Involving the Kids, page 71).

A fulfilling "job" for a Boxer can be as simple as "chief ball retriever."

Giving a Working Dog a Job to Do

Because the Boxer is truly a working breed, the benefits of training go a step further. The Boxer was bred to work closely with her handler (see History of the Boxer, page 6), and as a working breed, this innate characteristic is still very much a part of the Boxer. Give this breed a job to do and she will relish the opportunity to work with you. But what sort of job can you give this dog?

Training your Boxer new skills, such as basic or advance obedience, agility, carting, or tracking, for instance, can give your Boxer a real purpose for all her training. If you have the time, becoming involved in an activity in which your Boxer is apt to excel can further develop her. You will notice a difference in her heightened responses to you in everyday life, too. But don't fret if you don't have time for a more involved sport. Your Boxer will be completely happy to take on any job you might assign her, such as the enviable position of being "chief ball retriever" or "primary jogging companion."

2 *Understanding the Boxer*

As mentioned in the previous chapter, Boxers are working dogs. They and their progenitors for centuries before have been bred to work in a variety of jobs. Unlike other breeds, which were bred to work *independently* of their owners, such as livestock guardian breeds, sighthounds, etc., the Boxer was bred to work with and directly for his handler.

History of the Boxer

The Boxer was one of the very first breeds recognized by Germany as a police dog in the early 1920s. In order to earn this recognition, breeders had to show the dog's proficiency at performing a variety of tasks, including obeying basic commands, tracking, and protection work. These tests were the basis for today's Schutzhund tests. The Boxer was so proficient at this work that as a breed it had the greatest percentage of members pass the tests, second only to the Airedale.

War dogs. During World War I and World War II, Boxers served in a variety of war dog positions, including the role of a guard dog trained to prevent prisoners from passing messages to civilians, and a patrol dog that would alert his handler

to danger or help the soldier find his way from one location to another along dangerous and dark routes. Boxers were also used to run messages through battle-torn fields and under heavy fire. As an ambulance dog, the Boxer was used to find wounded soldiers and lead medics back to the wounded. (One Boxer received Germany's Iron Cross for saving so many lives during World War I.) In WWII, the Boxer's duties included running communications lines.

Service dogs. After the wars, Boxers continued to be used in a variety of close-working service jobs in both the United States and Europe. Today, in the United States, Boxers often can be seen as service dogs for the disabled, and as trained animal-assisted therapy dogs. In Europe, Boxers are used as guide dogs for the blind, and frequently are trained by volunteer organizations and the Red Cross in search and rescue work.

Police dogs. Though the Boxer is still listed as one of Germany's accepted breeds for police work, the German Shepherd and the Belgian Malinois are far more popular today. There's a common saying in Germany among K-9 officers: "In the time it takes to train one Boxer, an officer can train two German Shepherds." This is usually recanted with a smile and a shake of the head, and a further comment on the Boxer not being too serious about his tasks or "having too many jokes in his head." However, all this is noted with the qualifier that if an officer chooses to train a Boxer, perhaps because he or she has had experience with the breed, the *trained* police Boxer is a *very* good dog to have.

The key here is *trained*. Even among those who are experienced in training working dogs, the Boxer can still prove to be a challenge. For those who live, breathe, and *know* Boxers, the task may still be time consuming, but it is much simpler and extremely rewarding. The trick therefore, is to *understand* the Boxer.

Innate Instincts

The Boxer has many working dog characteristics for which he has been selectively bred for generations. Along with these working characteristics, there are also a few traits that are just, well, "pure" Boxer. Armed with a knowledge of working dog and pure Boxer traits, you will be better equipped to understand your own dog and modify your training methods to match his needs.

In other words, a Boxer is not a retriever disguised in a Boxer body. A Boxer is a Boxer, and training one with the same expectations you might have with another breed of dog simply won't work. It is a unique breed with its own strengths and weaknesses. Recognizing typical Boxer behavior will make you

more adept at handling and training this breed than the owner who has no real idea what to expect.

The following are some traits that are commonly associated with the Boxer breed. Again, there is variation from dog to dog, but most Boxers will display the majority of these characteristics.

High activity level/energy. The Boxer was bred for endurance. It was at one time expected to work beside its owner all day or as long as it was needed. Even today in Germany, one of the prerequisites for breeding is that the Boxer is able to display this working trait of endurance. As part of the German breeding suitability

Boxers are one of Germany's original breeds qualified to perform in police work.

test (which includes health tests, a passing conformation rating, and a performance test), the Boxer must be able to trot alongside a bicycle for roughly 12 miles (19 km) with only a few brief breaks.

So, what does this mean to the Boxer owner who is trying to train his or her dog? It means that you are working with a dog that has a healthy activity level. The Boxer is an extremely flashy, agile, and quick-footed dog when trained, but this breed can be a challenge to get focused as a young puppy or as an adolescent. To make training sessions more productive with younger Boxers, you must therefore consider your timing carefully. A brief romp to help blow off some steam could be just what it takes to get an energetic Boxer to concentrate on the task at hand; however, too much exercise and he may become too tired to focus on learning.

The Boxer is a very strong dog that is quite capable of dragging his owner if not trained to walk nicely.

Strength. The Boxer is an incredibly strong animal. It was originally bred to excel in work that requires raw, physical strength, such as protection work, in which the dog is trained to bite on command and not let go until given the command to release. The ability to hold onto a full-grown man is impressive enough, but to have the strength to be able to hold the man and keep him from running away takes an incredibly strong dog. The Boxer is this dog.

With this kind of strength, a pet Boxer can easily drag his owner down the street if he is not taught to *heel*, or at least walk without pulling. He can also, as an adult, literally use his strength to avoid doing anything he doesn't want to do, which is a problem with the dog that is not trained to obey your commands. Fortunately, Boxers are eager learners and want to please; they can learn virtually anything with gentle, positive reinforcement training (see Approaches to Training, page 15). If you use the right techniques, you'll be able to channel your Boxer's strength into very positive activities.

Courage. If there is one thing the Boxer is noted for as a breed, it is his great courage. The Boxer was bred to be a self-confident breed that could be both brave in the face of the most fearsome threat, and yet gentle and kindhearted with those he loves. Today, there is a range of temperaments among Boxers, with many that still possess this intrinsic courage and a natural instinct to guard their loved ones, home, and territory. There are also those that appear to be so outgoing that it is generally assumed they would lead a burglar to the jewels just to make friends. However, don't let this wonderful outward appearance fool you; behaviorists note that the friendly, confident dog is perhaps the best guardian of all. Your Boxer can be trusted with everyone but will know when you are truly threatened.

If your Boxer is a self-confident type and possesses great strength of mind, he is also likely to possess a great will. This does not necessarily mean that he will try to dominate you; however, he may certainly think his way of doing things makes more sense than yours. The self-confident, courageous Boxer requires a loving environment with an affirmative, patient owner who is willing to provide the structure and gentle but firm leadership this dog needs.

Intelligence. Combined with the Boxer's self-confidence, strong will, and courage is a great sense of cleverness. What this translates to is that he will remain two steps ahead of anything you can possibly envision. Did you ever think your Boxer would figure out how to get into the refrigerator? Open a door using a *round* doorknob? Jump the back fence, run around to the front door, and ring the doorbell? It's pretty much a given that your Boxer will think of several things that you could never have imagined. The Boxer's intelligence at solving problems is impressive. Their intelligence in creating *new* problems is also impressive. Just when you think you've got your dog to be consistent in his response to a command, watch out! He may think of something new to do, just to toss things up a bit.

For the Boxer owner, this could mean frustrating periods with your pet in which

> **Boxer Byte:** Every once in a while, you will find a Boxer that is fearful or timid. This can be a result of either an inherited temperament or poor early life experiences, such as lack of socialization. Or it could be a combination of both genetics and environment. Whatever the reasons for the fearfulness, this Boxer will need an experienced hand and some extra nurturing from the owner to provide an environment that will help develop him into a more self-assured dog.
>
> Many of these Boxers, once they learn to trust humans again and overcome any other fears they might have, can become excellent pets and even good competitors. (A top agility instructor noted that fearful dogs, once they've mastered several components of the agility test, often blossom with new self-confidence and literally become different dogs!)

you will be mentally taxed on problem solving with him. Maintaining a good sense of humor helps with this aspect of the Boxer, as does a generous dose of patience. It also helps to be familiar with potential Boxer antics while rearing him, so you can at least be close to predicting—and thus preventing—certain training challenges.

Close working. Boxers, as with many German breeds, were bred to work closely with their handler. They were not intended to be dogs that work independently of their master or at great distances from their handler. Boxers were developed to assist the handler in whatever job they were given to do and to be responsive to their master's commands.

The close-working trait of the Boxer coupled with his eagerness to please his owner, are good training characteristics

You never know what these Boxers will think of next . . .

to possess. These same traits, however, mean that he will never want to be far from his humans. He was not bred to be a loner; he thrives in the company of people. Therefore, if you cannot spend a lot of time with your pet or involve him in much of your daily activities, you are sure to experience behavior problems, namely the destruction of your home and yard. If you work with him and include him in all that you do, you will find his working traits are tremendous assets.

Clowning. The Boxer separates himself from many of the other working breeds in that he never takes life too seriously—ever. He is known to be a clown during all stages of life, from puppyhood to old age. This irrepressible characteristic of the Boxer knows no boundaries, even international ones. The most highly-titled Schutzhund Boxers in Germany have been known to "do the kidney bean" at the sight of the first person who *might* pet them.

Though this silliness and perpetual puppyhood might frustrate some trainers who expect all work and no play from their dogs, the true Boxer lover accepts this characteristic as part of the endearing qualities of the Boxer.

Channeling the Positives

With an understanding of how some of the Boxer's inherent traits may affect your training approach, it is equally important to be aware of some common training mistakes that owners sometimes make with their dogs. Though Boxers are

The Boxer is always looking for fun ways to play, and the more Boxers (generally) the merrier!

working dogs and can be trained for such serious, focused work as advanced obedience, tracking, and protection work, they are not a "hard headed" or a "thick-skinned" breed. Boxers are typically very responsive to their owner's corrections, so much so that a heavy hand can squash their inborn enthusiasm.

Once the joy of training is lost for a Boxer, it is very hard to regain; therefore, particularly if you are interested in competing in competitive events, you must take great care to maintain your Boxer's enthusiasm.

This also means that training sessions must be kept interesting and motivating. Though some dogs may willingly sit on command 100 times in a row, or fetch a ball for hours on end, this repetitive training will only bore your Boxer. When a Boxer becomes bored, watch out! The creativity (or "unlearning") starts.

Training sessions need to be kept brisk and relatively short until your Boxer advances in his training and matures to a level at which he willingly can focus for longer periods of time; however, you need to be cognizant of your pet's mental abilities and always end the training session *before* he becomes bored or tired. Puppies can receive a few minutes of training interspersed throughout the day, whereas, an adult may easily be able to focus for 20 minutes or longer, depending on the activity, the level to which the dog is currently trained, and the handler's skill in training.

In general, the Boxer is a wonderful and interesting breed to train. With a good grounding on Boxer behavior and an understanding of typical Boxer traits, you will be well equipped for modeling training methods to best meet your pet's needs.

3 *How the Boxer Learns*

To maximize the efficiency of your training and to minimize as many human errors as possible, it is important to understand a little about what is going on in your Boxer's head. Unfortunately, there is not a "Boxer language dictionary" available for sale—yet. But animal behaviorists and researchers have studied dog behavior extensively, and we do know quite a bit about how dogs communicate and learn.

The Concept of Learning from a Dog's View

First of all, dogs are very intelligent, but they do not learn in the same ways as humans. (And despite what your Boxer may have told you, she is *not* human.) For example, it is generally accepted that a dog cannot be taught to read, speak a human language in complete sentences (there has been at least one dog that reportedly could sing in Italian), or write. However, your Boxer has a *great* capacity to learn! And, what sets this breed apart from many others, is that she *wants* to learn. She wants to be your companion, your trusted friend, *your* Boxer. Learning the subtleties behind how your Boxer

learns what you teach her and how she learns from other dogs, can give your training abilities quite a boost.

Visual Communication

Research has shown that dogs are very visual. They are stimulated by what they see. This probably comes as no surprise to Boxer owners who are used to their dogs spotting and investigating every leaf, airplane, car, child, or any other object that moves. Dogs also look for and respond to visual cues, which means that much of the dog's "language" is visual. Dogs use their muzzles, ears, eyes, tails, and bodies to get their points across. These body cues can communicate a myriad of messages such as contentment, annoyance, submissiveness, and playfulness, as well as dominance and aggression.

Hand signals. Your movements are important to your dog. Visual cues such as hand signals are very effective in training dogs. (That's a tremendous plus if you've got a deaf Boxer!) Hand signals also always *sound* the same to a dog. Using hand signals in training, therefore, gives the dog a lot of consistency in training.

For example, if you've chosen to touch your chin for the *sit* command, no matter

Boxer Byte: Renowned canine-psychology researcher Stanley Coren, Ph.D., presents some interesting and rather intriguing theories regarding dog-dog communication in his recent book, *How to Speak Dog: Mastering the Art of Dog-Human Communication.* The type of ears best suited for communicating are natural prick ears, says Coren, with puppyish, lop ears in second place. In last place, is the closely cropped ear. Because of the artificial nature of this type of ear, Coren believes that the dog's hampered ability to show friendly positioning to other dogs could actually initiate aggressive behavior in other dogs. The longer, show crop is better than the shortly cropped guard-style ear, he says, because with more ear standing up, the dog can show ear "signals" more visibly. Further studies are needed to confirm this theory, but it is an interesting concept.

voice of a child trying to get a wild adolescent dog to sit may only have the effect of exciting the Boxer even more.

Body language. Beyond hand signals, the entire movement and silent language of your body are being watched and interpreted by your dog. For this reason, your body language is very important in training dogs. Your Boxer can see by the way you walk and by the expression on your face *precisely* how you feel, and she will quickly pick up on this mood. If you walk with a bounce, smile, and use your entire body to express your happiness with her, not only will she be more attentive, she will intuitively know she's doing a good job and you are pleased with her. If, however, you are scowling or stern with your facial expressions and your body is tense or without much expression,

The adeptness with which this deaf Boxer learns hand signals is due to all dogs' inherent ability to recognize and learn visual signals.

what kind of mood you are in when you give the command (perhaps grouchy from work or angry because your loving Boxer just polished off your lunch), the command looks and sounds the same. Hand signals also transfer well from person to person: You will find that your five-year-old can give a hand signal and have the dog obey, whereas, the higher-pitched she will quickly realize you are displeased and irritated, which will result in a confused and unhappy dog.

If you've had a bad day, wait until you're in a better mood to work with your dog. If you tend to be very reserved with your body language, work on smiling more and loosening up—your Boxer won't tell anyone how silly you can be!

Oral communication. Body language, of course, is not the only tool you can use to train your Boxer. Though it is not believed that dogs understand too many human words, they can understand enough words that a solid repertoire

Boxers enjoy physical and verbal praise, and will respond enthusiastically to these rewards.

can be taught successfully. The Boxer communicates with a wide variety of sounds; there's no mistaking what pleasure a Boxer expresses! Barking, growling, whining, snarling, and rumbling—that ultimate contentment sound of a Boxer about to drift off to sleep on a very comfy bed—are all part of the Boxer's repertoire of sounds used to speak to other dogs as well as to humans.

Most owners quickly pick up on the reason for the dog's sounds, though we don't exactly understand *what* our dogs are saying. Dogs, however, can learn to understand some of our language, say researchers, and tend to filter out the words that are important or pertain to them.

So how much can our dogs understand of what we are saying? Some psychologists believe dogs can learn to understand as many different words as a toddler, or roughly 200 spoken words. Still others believe that dogs can learn in excess of 300 words. Even if the experts are on the high end of reality, there's no reason why a dog can't understand a repertoire of 10 to 20 words that will be the basis for your commands. Of course, getting your Boxer to *respond* appropriately to these words lies in your training, which we will deal with shortly!

Age Counts

Boxer owners should also take into consideration the age of their dog when training her. The most distinct difference between puppies and adults is that puppies have difficulty focusing on any one thing for very long. Puppies benefit the most from many small, short training sessions or intermittent command work throughout the day (i.e., *"sit"* for a cookie, *"sit"* for her dinner bowl, *"sit"* before the door is opened, *"sit"* for a pat from the neighbor, etc.).

The adult Boxer has overcome a lot of the puppy's hampered ability to focus, but a young adult (12–24 months) can still be easily distracted in training. It's not that the ability to focus isn't there at this age; rather, it goes back to the discussion about the Boxer's intelligence and her tendency to become quickly bored. Learning must remain fast-paced, fun, and creative for any age Boxer. As long as you remain more interesting than the leaf falling from a nearby tree, you've got the situation under control.

Approaches to Training

Now that you know a bit about how your Boxer learns, it's time to learn what kind of training tools you have at your disposal and what works best with the Boxer. So, let's begin with what *doesn't* work: physical domination.

Physical Domination

Physical domination includes hitting, slapping, beating, pinning, "scruffing" (grabbing the dog by the skin on her neck and getting right into her face), and alpha rolling (forcing the dog into a submissive position on her back). These methods are *not* effective and accomplish nothing except, perhaps, to cause a dog that would never have bitten otherwise to bite in self-defense. *Abuse is not a teaching tool.*

Boxer Byte: As for tail docking, Coren says that a dog without a tail is simply not able to communicate efficiently with tail signals. (Coren lists 14 different tail positions used by dogs to communicate.) This inability, in turn, can hamper the docked dog's relationships with other dogs. In one study performed by Coren, it was found that dogs with docked tails were twice as likely to have aggressive encounters than dogs with tails. Though the docked dog itself may be trying to display friendliness (we can recognize that wiggling rear end!), other dogs may not be able to interpret these tail signals as clearly and may initiate aggression.

This Boxer's natural ears and full tail may help her communicate better with dogs and humans.

Unfortunately, there are still trainers in this world who will claim physical dominance is the only way to train some dogs; if you find one of these folks, run. Here's why.

Boxers are intelligent, trusting, and loyal creatures. Just like children, dogs can take only so much of any kind of abusive treatment before one of several things happens. The dog may become distrustful of all humans. She could become so fearful of her master that she might actually fear for her life and try to protect herself by biting. (This is not considered dominant behavior.) Or, if the Boxer is a self-assured, dominant type, attempts to manhandle the dog into submission will escalate the situation, not solve it. With any of these scenarios, nothing is accomplished. So, let it be said that if there is one way *not* to train a dog, it is with physical domination.

Negative Reinforcement

This type of training does work in a way, but it is not a preferred method. Prior to the 1980s, when the movement began toward positive reinforcement, training with negative reinforcement had been a widely accepted method of training, and people did get results and they did train dogs.

Technically speaking, negative reinforcement is the use of a verbal or physical correction when the dog makes a mistake. For example, if a dog lunges ahead of the handler, the quick uptake or "pop" of a metal choke chain is a negative reinforcement. The dog realizes quickly that if she lunges forward, she will get hurt—a little. So, by seeking to *avoid* punishment, this is how she learns.

Verbal negative reinforcement includes shouting *"No"* or *"Stop"* when your puppy starts to urinate on the carpeting. Your voice tells the puppy what you don't want her to do; however, your voice correction doesn't tell your puppy what you *want* her to do. Only your actions following this halting command, such as picking up the puppy and putting her outside, accompanied with praise or a treat, will tell her what you want her to do.

Unfortunately, negative reinforcement—particularly physical methods—lends itself to being a training tool that is often mishandled. Some owners take the corrections too far and are physically abusive with their dogs. Some dogs are so "soft" emotionally that a swift correction (verbal or physical) can literally crush their enthusiasm. Once enthusiasm is lost, it is rarely, if ever, regained.

Negative reinforcement, as mentioned above, can get results, but research has shown that both owners and dogs enjoy positive training methods much more. Additionally, some researchers have shown that positive training methods are generally faster in shaping behaviors and may have a greater rate of retention. Twenty years of use and continued evolvement have made positive reinforcement the preferred method of training today.

Positive Reinforcement

The key to this popular method of training is to set your dog up for success, limit her chances for failure, and reward her when she does a task correctly.

Boxer Byte: Many positive, motivational training methods use food as both a lure (i.e., to position the dog into a sit) and a reward; however, you may choose to use something different. It really depends on what your Boxer's strongest stimulus is. Is it food? Play? A ball? Your voice? Or, is it physical attention? Perhaps your Boxer will respond best to a combination of rewards, such as food, praise, and pats.

Items that can be used to reward your dog include treats, balls, verbal praise, physical praise, and even playtime with a tug toy. What type of positive reinforcement you use can greatly determine how quickly your dog learns and affect how eager she is to please you. For more information on rewards, see Reinforcements, page 56.

Toy rewards can be very effective training tools.

In the United States, the pioneers credited with developing positive, motivational training methods are veterinarian and animal behaviorist Ian Dunbar and scientist and animal trainer Karen Pryor. Working independently beginning in the 1980s, Dunbar and Prior are credited not only with presenting their methods of positive, motivational training, but also with being instrumental in the widespread adoption of this training method by trainers all over the country. The system is based on rewards, shaping, and fading.

Rewards. To use a positive, motivational training method successfully, the dog is rewarded for accomplishing the task you have asked of her, such as sitting on voice or hand command. Initially, the dog is rewarded with a treat *every* time she performs the new task correctly. Repetition plays a key part in her learning.

Shaping. Once the dog is performing the task with some consistency, and is being rewarded every time, then it's time for the next stage of positive reinforcement, which is called "shaping." In this stage, the rewards don't come every time the dog performs the task correctly; they come at variable times. Let's say the command is a *sit*. Instead of receiving a treat every time the dog sits, she is given a treat after every two, three, or four times

17

she sits. The dog doesn't know exactly when she will be rewarded, but she knows it will be soon.

Fading. The final stage of positive reinforcement is when the reward is given even less frequently, usually after a series of commands have been performed. This last stage is called "fading," because the reward is not as prominent with learned commands.

Training the Deaf Boxer

Deafness is part of the Boxer breed. As with other breeds that can have coats of pure white or white with patches of color, the Boxer has a genetic risk for bilateral

Training a deaf Boxer requires the use of visual commands, patience, and lots of love.

deafness, or deafness in both ears. This type of deafness is seen in Boxers with white or check (white with patches of color) coats, and is caused by the lack of pigment in the cells lining the dog's ears. There is no known way to correct this hearing loss.

Previously, deaf dogs were often euthanized because it was believed that the deaf dog was untrainable. Not so. And it doesn't take a special trainer, either. All that is needed is a slightly different form of training.

If you own a deaf Boxer, you will be able to teach your dog all the commands and tricks in this book with one basic variation: The method you will use for gaining your deaf dog's attention will be different. Since she is deaf, she cannot hear her name, the set-up cue used to let the dog know she must listen. The owner of the deaf Boxer must do something different to get the dog's attention: a stomp on the floor, a mild pagerlike buzz of an electronic collar, the flash of a penlight, or the toss of a beanbag across her line of vision.

Once the deaf dog's attention is gained, she is rewarded. Over time, the deaf Boxer will learn the cue to focus on her owner. When she understands the *look at me* signal, the owner can begin coupling this with training for as many commands as desired. The commands can be taught using food lures as outlined in this book coupled with hand signals, rather than voice commands.

Many owners use their own version of hand signals to communicate with their deaf dogs; some choose to use American Sign Language. The choice is really the owner's.

4 **House-training**

To be a successful house dog and a valued companion, your Boxer will need to be dependable in the house. He must learn to relieve himself outside and not in your living room or behind a couch.

Dogs are born with the inherent desire not to soil their dens or immediate sleeping areas. In order to house-train a dog, you must take his innate desire to not soil his bed and transfer this behavior to first one room, then several rooms, and eventually the entire home. This involves a great deal of patience, practice, timing, and consistency. Fortunately, house-training is something all Boxers, regardless of age, should learn readily and with few problems.

Despite this, one of the most frequently heard complaints among dog owners is: "I'm having difficulties house-training my dog!" The fault is rarely with the dog. As top-notch trainers know, if a dog is not learning a certain behavior, the fault usually lies with the trainer and not the dog. The same is true of house-training.

When a Boxer does not house-train easily, it is most often because the owner failed the dog in one of three ways: Either the owner did not understand the basic principles of house-training a young puppy or adult dog, could not meet the house-training needs and schedule of the

Boxer, or did not train the Boxer positively and/or with consistency.

Understanding Urges and Abilities

Boxers are noted for being a breed that house-trains at an early age. They tend to be even more meticulous in wanting to keep their living area clean than many other breeds. Some owners even refer to the Boxer's cleanliness as "catlike." The Boxer puppy begins to show this inherent fastidiousness as early as five weeks of age, when he is careful to relieve himself away from his mother and littermates' nest. This desire to remain clean continues as the puppy matures, so if you are careful to maintain and build on your Boxer's desire to be a clean dog, house-training should be a snap.

Older Boxers can be house-trained, too, with relatively few problems. Often, untrained adults are much faster to house-train than puppies. Since healthy adult dogs have full control over their bladder and bowel movements, they are capable of "holding" for hours at a time and are less likely to make mistakes.

The Boxer puppy has a natural instinct not to soil his den.

Sniffing, circling, or squatting are all signs of a need to "go." (Male puppies will also squat.)

Knowing the signs. Whether you are training a puppy or an adult, it is important to recognize when your Boxer needs to relieve himself. Adults and puppies will need to eliminate immediately upon waking in the morning, within a half hour after eating, following periods of play or other physical activities, and at least once or more during the day. They also need to relieve themselves just before retiring for the night.

Young puppies (8 to 16 weeks) do not have as much control as older puppies or adult dogs, and will need to relieve themselves at additional times throughout the day. (Young male puppies may "dribble" across the floor when they are particularly excited. Young male and female puppies may urinate in a submissive gesture.) In other words, virtually *any time* is a potential time to urinate, and many times are opportunities to defecate. You can figure that a young puppy will need to relieve

himself roughly every two to three hours throughout his waking and busy hours.

Fortunately, the Boxer puppy gains control fairly quickly. Bowel control comes first followed by bladder control. Around 14 weeks of age, the Boxer puppy usually already has control of his bowels, and is on the verge of controlling his bladder for longer periods of time. By 16 weeks of age, a puppy should be capable of sleeping comfortably through the night without any accidents.

Warning Signs

Before the Boxer puppy reaches the magical four-month stage of control and for many months thereafter, the owner must be particularly watchful. In addition to giving the puppy ample opportunities to urinate or defecate, the owner must learn to recognize the "I need to go" signs of a puppy and quickly take him outside to relieve himself.

For those who have not had a puppy in a long time, the signs of the puppy needing to urinate or defecate are the same as for an adult dog: He will halt his current activity and sniff the ground or circle the floor. With puppies, you've got to be quick! Their sequence of "preelimination" events can occur so rapidly that the owner has little or no time to prevent the puppy from relieving himself in the wrong place. Sometimes the puppy, similar to a busy toddler at play, may not even realize he has to "go" until it is too late to reach the appropriate location. For this reason, a very young puppy should be allowed only in areas of the home that have been floored with a surface that can be cleaned easily without any residual scent, such as tile or vinyl. Avoid carpeted floors that are hard to clean and tend to retain odors.

The Basic Principle of Praise

Once you understand the limits of your Boxer and are better able to prevent accidents, the next basic concept of successful house-training is knowing when to praise, when to scold, and when not to do anything.

Rewarding the puppy or dog when he relieves himself outside or in a designated area is very important. The more times you can reward your Boxer for urinating or defecating outside, the faster he will learn that this is where you want him to go all the time.

Boxer Byte: A Boxer that is raised in deplorable conditions and comes in constant contact with his own feces and urine may develop into what is referred to by some as a "dirty dog." Once a Boxer becomes a dirty dog, he can be difficult to house-train. Because he seemingly doesn't mind the smell of his eliminations near where he sleeps or eats, confinement to a small area to prevent inappropriate eliminations is not effective in itself.

The situation is easily preventable—but can it be corrected? What if you adopt a Boxer that has been raised in a situation such as this? For most Boxers, the innate desire to be clean will prevail, say rescue workers. And once he is cleaned up (sometimes for the first time in his life) and provided with a clean area in which to sleep and relax, the rest comes very naturally. Vigilance in providing frequent opportunities for the Boxer to relieve himself (just as with a young puppy) is recommended in the early stages of house-training for this mistreated Boxer.

However, when praising your Boxer for eliminating, don't get overly excited. This is the time for a gentle, soft-spoken, *"Good dog. Good job,"* and a small treat immediately after he has chosen an

Mild scolding is only appropriate when the puppy is caught in the act—as with this young female.

For example, if you suddenly discover a wet spot on your carpet and call your Boxer over to the evidence on your carpet, and *then* scold him, what have you accomplished? Well, the last thing he remembers doing is coming when you called him. So, instead of piecing together that you are really angry about the wet spot, he thinks he's getting a tongue-lashing for coming when you called him. Now guess what? Instead of teaching him that relieving himself on the carpet is a "no-no," you've just taught him that he will be punished for coming when he is called.

Roughness. Other rough actions such as trying to "collar" your dog and pull him over to the scene of the crime won't work much better. Again, your intelligent Boxer won't associate this scolding with the accident he had hours, minutes, or even seconds ago. Instead, he will associate "bad things" whenever you walk up to him and reach for his collar. Then, the next time you reach for your dog, watch how fast and far away he will jump out of your reach!

So, what do you do when you discover that while you weren't looking, he relieved himself in the *wrong* place? Nothing. That's right. You do absolutely nothing. Simply take him outside, praise him gently but profusely when he relieves himself in the appropriate place, and then quietly clean up the accident.

The only time it is appropriate to mildly scold a dog with house-training is *when you catch him in the act itself*. Usually a good shriek, which is a natural human response to a puppy or dog soiling the carpet or furniture, is enough to

appropriate place. If you let out loud praise while your Boxer is relieving himself, he is likely to stop what he is doing and come running to figure out what is so wonderful—and the concept of the praise for eliminating may be temporarily lost.

Timing. As for any scolding, gone is the old concept of dragging the dog or puppy to the site of an accident long after the actual act occurred and verbally or physically punishing the dog. Bad, bad, bad owner! Studies have shown that this accomplishes nothing, except for perhaps worsening the situation. Your Boxer will associate his scolding with the most recent event he has experienced, *not* the actual act of urinating or defecating.

startle your Boxer and cause him to stop "midstream." If he is a young puppy, quickly pick him up without any anger and carry him outside, repeating the command, *"Outside."* If he is an adult, a *"No"* may be in order to stop the action, followed by a quick ushering of the dog outside, along with the command, *"Outside."*

Note: If your backyard has a patio or a deck, make sure you guide your puppy all the way to the grass to relieve himself. You want to make sure that he understands at an early age that the cement or brick patio or the wooden deck are *not* places he can eliminate.

Once the Boxer is outside, wait until he begins relieving himself. This may take a little while, since he is already upset and realizes that he has made you unhappy. Try to be calm and patient and forget for a minute what he just did. (Remember. It was an accident!) Once he settles down, he should quickly complete his duties. When this happens, praise him gently and reward him with a little treat.

Cleaning Up Mistakes

Since dogs tend to eliminate in areas in which they can find their scent, it is critical to eliminate any remnants of an accident in areas you do not want your Boxer to revisit. Unfortunately, his acute sense of smell will detect even minuscule amounts or urine or feces, so it is particularly important to clean up any accidents immediately and thoroughly.

The first rule of cleaning up mistakes is to remove as much of the offending matter as possible. For urine, blot up as much of the liquid as you can using paper towels. If your Boxer has defecated, pick up the stool carefully and remove all visible solid material.

Once all visible urine or feces is out of the way, use a pet stain and odor remover to neutralize the spot. There are specialized cleaners that use enzymes to break down the organic material in urine and stool, which can be very successful in removing all traces of smells.

Boxer Byte: Owners are often tempted to use household cleaning products to clean their Boxers' mistakes, then they are puzzled as to why the treated area actually smells *worse* than it did before. The reason is that many household cleaning products contain ammonia. Ammonia is very effective in killing off germs; however, it happens to be one of the chemicals contained in dog's urine. When used in an attempt to clean a urine spot, the dog still smells ammonia, which could be confused with urine.

A homemade cleaner that can be used with relative success is white vinegar. Use a mixture of 20 percent white vinegar to 80 percent water. Be sure to test the mixture on a hidden spot of your carpet to check for color fastness.

Boxer Byte: Occasionally, an adopted adult dog that has not been exposed to a constant water supply will gorge on water as if this water is the last drink he will have for days. This is not healthy, of course, and it also wreaks havoc with house-training because the dog will need to urinate at unpredictable times and in copious amounts.

If your Boxer tends to gorge on water, the first thing you should do is consult with your veterinarian and rule out any health problems that might cause an insatiable thirst, such as diabetes. Once thirst-causing illnesses are ruled out, you can begin working on acclimating him to a constant supply of water.

One method involves supplying the gorging Boxer with a small amount of water at all times. Allow him to drink the small amount until it's gone, and then refill the water bowl with another small portion an hour later, continuing throughout the day. Eventually, he will realize that water will always be available, and he doesn't need to drink it all at once. Old habits can be hard to break, so some patience is needed in this situation. If this gorging habit is not adjusted within two or three weeks, seeking additional advice from your veterinarian, or even possibly a certified animal behaviorist, would be advisable.

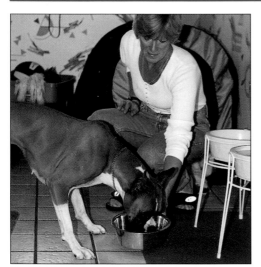

Establishing a regular eating routine (meals at set time) will help your Boxer settle into a predictable elimination pattern.

When cleaning urine spots in carpets, make sure you have used enough of the cleaning liquid to reach all of the urine. This may mean soaking the carpet thoroughly to reach the pad and the subflooring. The amount of urine that was allowed to penetrate the carpet's surface will dictate how much pet stain and odor remover you may have to use.

The Importance of a Routine

In order to cut down on the potential number of accidents your Boxer may have over the course of his house-training, it is important to establish an eating and walking routine. The more regular and consistent you are with his feeding and walking schedule, the more likely he is to fall into a regular and predictable pattern of relieving himself.

As mentioned earlier in this chapter, both puppies and adults will need to relieve themselves shortly after eating meals. Knowing this, you can control this factor by providing your pet with meals scheduled at the same times every day (puppies three times a day, adults twice a day). A walk or an outside opportunity for him to defecate should be scheduled within a half hour after eating. Free-feeding, or allowing him to eat at will throughout the day, should be avoided since he will then need to defecate at various times throughout the day and perhaps even during the night.

Limiting Water

In order to control the frequency of urination, some house-training programs recommend limiting a puppy or dog's supply of water to the same periods in which he eats, and then picking up this water at other times throughout the day. This is *not* advisable. Fresh, cool water should not be withheld from your Boxer and should be available throughout the day, but water *can* be picked up after approximately two hours before his last opportunity to relieve itself at night. Limiting a dog's water supply to only a few times a day, however, may encourage gorging or drinking copious amounts of water in a short period of time, which is thought to be one of several reasons Boxers bloat. (Unless treated immediately by a veterinarian, bloat is often fatal.)

Fresh water should be available at all times; however, you can pick up water two hours before your dog's last trip outside at night.

Putting It All Together

Two strategies that are commonly used to facilitate house-training include crate training or paper training. Depending on your long-term plans about how you'd like your dog to relieve himself, either method can work. Crate training is the preferred method for most dog owners and works well with Boxers of virtually all ages. Paper training is a method primarily reserved for young puppies.

Crate Training

The basic idea behind crate training is that the dog is kept in his crate whenever he cannot be watched closely by his owner. As noted earlier, because Boxers have a strong aversion to wetting or soiling their own area, they will refrain from relieving themselves as long as they can while they are in their crate.

With crate training, it is important that you always remember to crate the dog *only* after he has thoroughly relieved himself. To do otherwise would be setting him up for failure. Also, you need to realize that there is a limit to how many hours a Boxer can be crated at one stretch of time. Crating should be done *only* when you cannot watch him—not when you don't *feel* like watching him. There's a difference. The former makes for successful crate training, the latter for a physically and mentally unhealthy, cooped-up dog.

So, how long can you crate a him? During the dog's active, day hours, he should never be crated beyond his physical limits to "hold." A good rule of thumb for figuring crate limits is to take his age in months, and add one hour up to a maximum range of seven or eight hours. For example, an eight-week-old puppy should not be crated for more than three hours at a time (two months plus one hour equals three hours). A six-month-old puppy, however, should be able to handle seven hours in a crate.

No dog, should be confined for more than seven or eight hours during the day without the opportunity for a walk and some exercise. The Boxer's total crate time in a 24-hour period should not exceed 10 hours, if possible. This, of course, is difficult if the owner works long hours and no one is home. However, there are solutions to every situation (see Home Schooling, page 32).

During periods in which your Boxer is confined, make sure to provide him with a few safe toys—such as tough rubber balls that can be stuffed with treats or nylon bones—that will keep him happily occupied for periods of time. (Do not give him squeaky toys, rawhides, hooves, or bones from chicken or other meats that can be easily destroyed or bitten up into chunks. These chews could pose choking hazards.)

Of course, crate training works only if your Boxer enjoys sleeping and relaxing in his crate. Most Boxers readily accept crate confinement within a day or two if the crate is the proper size, is comfortably lined or padded, and if he is consistently rewarded with a treat and praised for entering the crate. The crate should never be used as punishment.

Size. For a full-grown adult, the crate should be large enough for the dog to stand up, turn around, and lie down comfortably. Most Boxers will comfortably fit in a large crate, measuring roughly 24 inches wide × 36 inches deep × 26 inches high (61 × 91 × 66 cm). Smaller Boxers may fit a medium crate comfortably, and an exceptionally tall Boxer may require an extra-large size crate.

A puppy, of course, does not require an adult-size crate—at first. In fact, if the crate is to be used for house-training purposes, a much smaller crate is necessary. If you purchase an adult-size crate for a puppy, the puppy will have enough room in the crate to relieve himself in the corner and then lie safely away from the mess. Unfortunately, this sets your house-training efforts back a step because the puppy isn't taught to restrain its bowel or bladder movements.

With that said, you can do one of two things: First, you can purchase or borrow a smaller crate that fits the puppy for his first month or two, and then purchase a full-size crate when the puppy is five or six months old. Another option would be to buy a specially designed partition for your puppy's crate that makes a puppy-size crate out of an adult-size kennel. Whether you partition a larger crate or purchase or borrow a smaller crate, make sure the puppy's space is large enough for the puppy to stand, turn around, and lie down.

Boxer Byte: A crate is a very safe way to transport a dog in the car. The use of a crate in the home can help reduce separation anxiety, prevent destructive behavior, and keep a curious Boxer from getting into dangerous household items.

Crate types. Crates come in three styles: a hard shell, plastic crate; a wire, mesh style; and a soft, tentlike crate. All styles have their advantages, and whatever style you choose for your Boxer is mostly a matter of personal (and Boxer) preference.

1. The hard-shell plastic crate provides a more "denlike"feeling, but it has less ventilation than a mesh-style crate, which shouldn't be a problem in the

Types of crates (l to r): plastic, wire mesh, and a flexible, tentlike crate.

Baby gates, or gates made specifically for dogs, can be used to keep a Boxer in a specific room during house-training.

home but could be a problem if the crate is used in the back of a van or SUV with poor air circulation. The hard-shell kennel is the type that can be approved for air transportation should you ever need to ship your Boxer. These crates generally break down into two large pieces, so storing them takes up room. Also, cleaning up after an accident in this type of crate is generally easy; however, large messes will involve taking the crate apart and hosing it down in the backyard, in addition to scrubbing out every crack and fissure in the molded plastic.

2. The wire mesh crate is easy to break down and carry if it is a collapsible model. Cleaning out a mesh crate is simple, too, as the bottom pan slides out. Because the crate is mesh, the dog has a 360-degree view of his world and won't miss any action. Some dogs do not like the openness of the crate, while others may pull things in through the mesh, such as any blanket wrapping the crate. This crate is also not approved for airline travel.

3. The third type of crate is a new tentlike crate that is constructed of plastic mesh and PVC tubing. The advantages to this type of crate are that it is feather light and folds down to the equivalent of a few hollow tubes. The downside to this crate is that it is not airline approved, and a dog can very easily chew through the mesh panels. This crate could make

a good "second" crate, one that you could use after your Boxer is crate trained in either a wire or plastic crate.

If you are adopting an adult Boxer, consult with the rescue about what type of crate the dog is used to and accepts. If your Boxer is used to a certain kind of crate, why mess with a good thing?

If you are purchasing or already own a Boxer puppy, he will most likely adapt to whatever style of crate you like the best. However, you might consider consulting your breeder for some input as to what type of crate his or her dogs seem to enjoy more.

Comfort. For bedding, be sure to use materials that are inexpensive and either washable, such as old towels or blankets, or disposable, such as shredded newspapers. This will save a lot of frustration and expense in replacing bedding materials every time your Boxer has an accident. When he has mastered crate training, then you can consider more permanent bedding, such as specially made pads or fluffy dog beds, *if* your Boxer doesn't show a tendency to shred bedding!

Crate placement. Your Boxer's crate should be in the center of activity in your home. In this way, even when he is crated, he feels included in the household activities. The kitchen, breakfast room, or family room may be good locations in your home, depending on your lifestyle. At night, be sure to bring your Boxer—and his crate—to your bedroom.

Never banish the dog and crate to the basement or some other distant and lonely place. Boxers are true "people" dogs and separating them from people upsets them greatly, not to mention the fact that it takes a step back in their socialization process (see Socialization, pages 37–44). Also, make sure small children know the crate rules: No poking fingers or sticks into the crate; no banging toys on the roof or walls of the crate, and no sharing the crate. The crate is the Boxer's safe place and children should stay out.

Moving beyond the crate. When introducing your Boxer to larger spaces, it is wise to make this introduction in stages. For example, the first area to enlarge his privileges to might be the kitchen. The floor in this room is usually an easy-to-clean surface, so if there is an accident, it can be cleaned up efficiently. Place the crate in the kitchen and then use dog gates or baby gates to block all exits to other rooms and hallways. After the puppy has thoroughly relieved himself outside, allow him a short period of play in the kitchen. If he gets excited, take him outside and allow him to relieve himself again. The goal here is to *avoid* an accident in the kitchen area and to praise continued successes outside. When you can't watch your puppy in the kitchen, crate him until you can.

Once he has proven he is trustworthy in the kitchen, with no mistakes for a week or more, and when he is at *least* four months old, you may want to introduce another room. Make sure your Boxer is well walked and totally "empty" before introducing him to a new room. Again, watch him like a hawk. If he shows *any*

Boxer Byte: The easiest way to train your Boxer that he should eliminate *now*, is to give him a command. Yes, Boxers can learn to relieve themselves on command! To teach this convenient command, begin by saying the chosen phrase, such as "Go potty," or "Find a spot," when he is already relieving himself. Reward him with praise and a treat.

Also, when you are taking your Boxer out for a "relief" walk, don't walk. That's right. Go briskly to the designated area in which you want your dog to relieve himself and stand still. Allow him to circle around you, but don't allow him the option of going much farther. When he finally begins to relieve himself, reinforce the command and praise, praise, praise! Eventually, you will be able to walk to virtually any place and ask your Boxer to relieve himself. (This command is also very convenient while traveling.)

signs of eliminating in this new room, take him outside immediately and encourage him to relieve himself.

Prevention of *any* accidents and the reinforcement of proper eliminations are the quickest way to succeed when expanding the dog's safe zones. Any mistake made during house-training is a step back and can leave a permanent scent marker for your dog. The more vigilant you are and the more opportunities you

have to reward and praise the dog for good behaviors, the more success you will have with your dog.

Paper Training

Before crate training became popular, most owners taught their dogs to eliminate outside by what is referred to as paper training. This method has been used successfully by many dog owners, and if done properly, may be efficient for *some* Boxer owners *in some cases*.

Be forewarned, however, that when using the paper training method of house-training, there tends to be a greater margin of error—more "mistakes"—in the home before the dog masters the concept of going outside to relieve himself. The reason for this is that traditional paper training is really a two-step training process: First the puppy or dog must learn to eliminate *only* on the papered areas of a room. Then he must learn *not* to eliminate in the room, but only outside. It is often this transition from the first learning concept to the second that causes many dog owners trouble. Some dogs, after having learned that relieving themselves inside is acceptable, have difficulties understanding why they should relieve themselves outside.

To have a greater success rate with this house-training method, paper training should be used only as a "safety net" for the Boxer, not as an excuse to be less active in the dog's house-training. (It's easy to become lax when paper training a small puppy because the messes are small and can be picked up with the papers.)

The same principles and level of effort to prevent accidents in crate training need to be applied to paper training.

Papering. To house-train a Boxer using the paper training method, your first step is to choose a room that is suitable for this purpose. The kitchen usually works out well because it is centrally located—the puppy or adult never feels isolated—and the floor is generally of a material that is nonporous and cleans easily.

1. Once you've selected the room, make sure you have all exits safely blocked using dog gates or baby gates to keep the Boxer in this room only. Then place a thick layer of newspapers over *the entire floor*.
2. As with crate training, the dog should be fed, exercised, and allowed to relieve himself on a very regular schedule to avoid mishaps on the papered floor. Even though there are papers on the floor to catch accidents, you should not become lazy or inattentive to your puppy's needs. If he shows signs of needing to relieve himself, rush him outside with the command *"Outside,"* and praise him profusely when he relieves himself. Praise and reward *every* outside success.
3. As the puppy grows older, remove more and more papers from the floor until only one corner of the room still contains papers. If the Boxer has been using the papers to relieve himself, he will generally seek out these papers no matter where they are placed. Owners of many toy and small breeds use paper

training as a way to "litter" train their dogs and never attempt to make a transfer to the outside. Because of the Boxer's size, allowing a full-grown dog to relieve himself indoors is out of the question, so the final transfer to the outside must be made.

4. When you have worked your way down to a single, small area of the room that is papered, and your Boxer is old enough that he can be expected to "hold" for however many hours you are gone at a time, take these papers outside, with some scent remaining on them, and place them in the grass with the Boxer watching. He should then be allowed to sniff this new placement of the papers and encouraged to eliminate. Pick up and throw away the papers.
5. Be sure to leave an area outside in the grass with a bit of scent to help your dog connect that the backyard is where he should be going. Continue to praise him every time he relieves himself in the appropriate place.

Dog doors. One way to facilitate the learning processes involved in paper training is to consider installing a dog door from the kitchen, or whatever room you are using for house training, to the backyard. The dog door allows the dog to go outside to relieve himself whenever he needs to, whether or not you are home. In the early stages, you will need to continue to praise and reward him for going outside to relieve himself; however, within a relatively short period of time, he will jump through the door whenever he needs to.

31

Home Schooling

Common House-training Problems

Problem. *Whenever I let my Boxer puppy into the family room, he runs to the same spot behind the couch and urinates. What should I do?*

Solutions. This common problem usually occurs when an owner trusts the Boxer a little too soon with a little too much. First, the owner should thoroughly clean the area to which the puppy is running. This spot is attractive to the dog because it has a lingering scent. If the scent is into the carpet pad—or even the subflooring—this will need to be treated to remove the scent. Second, the owner should "block" this spot, which may be as simple as dragging the couch over the area that the puppy likes to use. Dogs also do not like to relieve themselves near their food, so feeding the puppy in this area may also be an option. Third, the owner should restrict the puppy from this room *unless two things have occurred*: 1) the puppy has totally relieved himself immediately before entering the room, and 2) the owner can provide the puppy with his or her undivided attention and watch for "warning" signs of the puppy's need to relieve himself.

Problem. *My Boxer was house-trained, but now he is urinating in his crate.*

Solutions. Have you changed any part of your routine recently? Sometimes owners "forget" the needs of their well-trained Boxers and start to become lax in their feeding, walking, and exercising schedule, or simply begin asking too much from their Boxers. If his routine has not been changed and he is suddenly urinating in his crate or elsewhere in the home, schedule an appointment with your veterinarian. There are many diseases that can cause excessive urination.

Problem. *My male Boxer is marking my living room couch.*

Solutions. If an adolescent or adult male is marking one particular piece of furniture, make it inaccessible to the dog—*unless you are present and watching*. Catching the dog in the act may put an end to this action. Also, make sure to thoroughly clean the furniture to remove all traces of the dog's scent.

If these actions fail, and if your Boxer is not neutered, you may want to consider having him altered. Researchers report that up to 60 percent of males with territorial problems stop this behavior when they are altered. Serious cases of marking may require other interventions, such as certain medications approved for lessening territorial behaviors.

Problem. *My Boxer won't alert me when he has to go outside, he just finds a spot in another room.*

Solutions. Thoroughly clean all "accidents" in the home and start over with the Boxer's house-training. A dog that does not signal an owner that he needs to go outside has not learned the basics of house-training. The use of a crate will facilitate the "alerting" portion of this training; the Boxer will not want to soil his area and will typically bark or cry when he needs to relieve himself. Once trained to alert you when in a crate, his house-training gradually can be broadened to include a room at a time—under your watchful eye. When you can't keep a close eye on the dog or if you are involved in another task, he should be returned to his crate, or kept on a leash tied to your belt. The leash will prevent any "dashing off" by the Boxer and will help him to alert his owner to any outside needs.

Problem. *My wife and I are gone all day. How can we possibly house-train our Boxer?*

Solutions. Until the Boxer reaches seven or eight months of age—when he can "hold" for seven or eight hours at a time—working owners need to be a little creative and come up with daytime solutions for their Boxers-in-training. One solution is to take a lunch break at home. This will provide him with roughly half an hour of exercise, attention, and an opportunity to relieve himself.

If you live too far away for this to be feasible, consider having a trusted neighbor, relative, or retiree to help with Boxer duties during the day. If you have a fenced backyard, the duties will be as simple as letting the dog out for half an hour, a little bit of play, and then re-kenneling the dog. Pet sitters are also available in many areas of the country, and can be hired for these same services.

If you have a backyard and a "safe" room leading to this backyard, you may want to consider a dog door to this area (see Dog Doors, page 31). Dog doors are a terrific way to allow your Boxer free access to the outdoors without relegating them to severe summer or winter temperatures.

Problem. *My elderly Boxer has started to urinate on himself when he sleeps. What can I do?*

Solutions. Incontinence at an advanced age is not a problem of humans alone! Silver Boxers can also suffer from incontinence. To determine if this is the problem, your Boxer should be thoroughly examined by a veterinarian to rule out any possible illnesses. If he is otherwise healthy, there are several things an owner can do.

First, the Boxer's pre-nighttime water intake can be restricted, just as it would be for a bed-wetting toddler. Second, his bedding can be changed to a specialized surface designed for incontinent dogs. The structure involves a raised grid that allows urine to go to the bottom of the crate and away from the dog. There are also pads that accomplish this. And third, there are medications available to help with incontinence. Your veterinarian can tell you if your silver Boxer can benefit from one of these drugs.

If a trusted Boxer begins to soil his crate, consult with a veterinarian for possible health problems.

If you are considering installing a dog door, keep in mind that the indoor portion of your home still needs to be an area of confinement for the dog. The indoor area should not be too large; just because the Boxer *can* go outside anytime to relieve himself doesn't mean he *will*. If you have other adult dogs in the home, however, you will be amazed at how quickly your puppy follows the adult dogs' lead and learns to hop through the door to relieve himself outside.

The confinement area needs to be small enough that the Boxer considers it "home." It also needs to be an area that is easily cleaned. (Keep in mind that whatever room the dog door leads to will see a lot of traffic, including muddy Boxer paws, unearthed chew toys, and other such debris and dirt.) The dog door is not an instant house-training fix, but it does facilitate learning in many cases.

Overcoming Lifestyle Complications

In a perfect puppy world, a Boxer owner would live at home and would attend to the puppy's needs day and night. If this were the case, house-training would be completed in short order and the whole process would theoretically involve no accidents.

But this isn't a perfect world. With dual-income families, many times the Boxer puppy or adult is left alone during the day and supervision can be given only in the evenings and at night. Other Boxer owners live in apartments or condominiums with

no backyard. Both situations are manageable; they just take a bit more effort from the owner.

Latchkey Boxers. For the Boxer that is left alone most of the day, you will need to create a situation in which he can use a dog door to a confined, safe area or a fenced backyard, or make arrangements to have him attended to periodically through the day.

If you have an adult dog you are trying to house-train, a midday break should be sufficient. If you can dash home on your lunch hour, or hire a pet walker to walk him, the adult dog should be happy until you can rejoin him in the evening.

If you have a puppy, you will need to make more visits home, or hire someone to do this for you. If you walk, feed, and then walk your puppy again before you leave for work at 7:00 A.M., your puppy will need relief by 9:00 or 10:00 A.M. He will then need to be fed again at noon, and walked. Three o'clock would be the next break for this little fellow and then again at 6:00 P.M. when you walk through the door and before you feed the puppy supper. Additional walks at 8:00 P.M. and 10:00 P.M. would be advisable to make sure the puppy is completely empty before curling up for the night.

Older puppies (6 months and up) should manage with one or two relief visits during the day.

Apartment dwellers. If you rent an apartment or live in a condominium, you very likely do not have a backyard and must rely on walking your Boxer to allow him to relieve himself. If this is the case, leash-training him immediately is particularly important (see Walk Nicely, page 72). It is also important that your Boxer can differentiate between a nice, long walk and the "relief" walk in which you want him to go right now, right here. For this, you'll need to train him with the *potty* command (see Boxer Byte, page 30).

City dawg. Some Boxer owners do not have the convenience of having a patch of grass for their dogs' use and must "curb" their dogs. Though this sounds difficult, it just takes practice. Many urban dogs can be taught to "curb" if this is the only area in which they have an option of relieving themselves.

When walking your Boxer, watch for signs that he may need to relieve himself. Move him quickly to the street side of the curb. While he is relieving himself, be sure to give him the *potty* command and then praise him gently. With some repetition, your Boxer will be able to "curb" quite well.

Note: Picking up after your dog is very important. When taking walks be sure to carry leftover plastic grocery bags or sandwich bags. To pick up a "deposit," turn the bag inside out around your hand, pick up the stool, and flip the bag over your hand. Seal and throw away in an appropriate receptacle.

5 *Socialization*

Is a good-natured, happy, well-adjusted Boxer the result of nature or nurture? It's much like the chicken and the egg question in that no one has a definitive answer but *everyone* has an opinion! So what's the right answer?

Opinions aside, and avoiding the chicken and egg question entirely, a dog's temperament and resulting behaviors are believed by animal behaviorists to be the result of both nature, through genetics, and nurture, through life experiences. Where the water gets muddied is in determining specifically *how much* influence genetics and environment have on the final outcome of a dog's temperament.

It is commonly accepted that a puppy is not born with an entirely "clean slate." Long before the puppy is whelped, she is genetically predisposed to have certain characteristics. Whether she reaches her full genetic potential is, however, dependent on her environment—how she is raised, nurtured, and shaped. Most animal behaviorists seem to feel that dogs—puppies and young dogs in particular—are very impressionable and moldable. Some experts estimate that the dog's environment, or nurturing, influences up to 40 percent of the dog's final temperament.

So in theory, a puppy that is predisposed to be aggressive toward other dogs *could* be raised in an environment that

would suppress this genetic tendency. In theory, too, it could be possible that a puppy that is predisposed to be gentle and loving could become an aggressive dog if she is exposed to a severe environment.

So, why are the genetics of temperament and the influences of learning environments so important to the Boxer owner? Because it explains why even if a Boxer puppy comes from parents with extremely nice temperaments, it is not a guarantee that the puppy will develop into a model Boxer. The "environment" and life experiences you provide your Boxer will, however. If you take care to provide an environment that is safe and full of positive experiences, she will be well on her way to becoming a "social" animal.

In the Beginning . . .

Some research indicates that the shaping of your Boxer's temperament may begin before she is actually born. Recent studies indicate that factors such as the position of the puppy in the mother's uterus and the mother's physical and mental state can affect the puppy's behavioral development.

Soon after birth, the puppy goes through an important phase of development with her mother and littermates. During this time, many of the puppy's

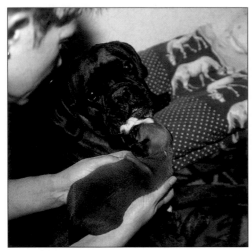

The temperament of the puppy's dam and the role of the breeder in nurturing the puppy play key roles in the puppy's future temperament.

"dog" behaviors are learned. It is also a time during which the puppy develops much of her trust of humans. For this reason, it is critical that puppies are handled gently and given a lot of human attention from birth. To raise them away from humans (i.e., in the backyard or in a kennel) is to deprive them of this contact, which is thought to result in the potential development of serious behavioral problems as the puppy matures.

Additionally, it is important not to separate the puppy from her mother too soon. Though some breeders will sell their puppies at six and seven weeks, research shows that puppies removed before the age of eight weeks may suffer from a host of problems later on, including, fear aggression, dog-dog aggression, and possibly a lack of bite inhibition.

So, out of all this, basically what is important to the Boxer owner is that the owner:

■ understands the important role the breeder plays in beginning the development of the puppy's human and canine socialization skills (and selects a puppy from a breeder who also understands his or her responsibilities); and

■ shouldn't be in a rush to bring home a puppy. Those extra days or weeks with her mother and littermates are very important to the future development of the dog.

Socialization with People

Once your puppy is home, she is in a critical socialization period. For about a month, or until the age of roughly 12 weeks, the experiences that your puppy lives through are thought to weigh heavily on how your puppy develops mentally and emotionally. One of your responsibilities during this time—and for the months following, is to socialize your Boxer with people. No matter how happy and sociable a puppy is, if she is kept in virtual isolation alone with her owner, there is a strong possibility that as an adult dog she will not respond appropriately with strangers either in the home or out and about in public.

With the legal liabilities that are present today, not working with your Boxer to ensure she is friendly with all types of people is a serious mistake. Boxers are incredibly strong for their size and have a powerful bite. Fortunately, by nature they are a gregarious sort and have an affinity toward loving all people, but don't take for granted that this nature will develop with your puppy. As the Boxer continues to climb in popularity, there will be increasing opportunities for genetically poor temperaments to creep into the breed.

So, even if you've purchased your puppy from the best of breeders and from the friendliest of Boxer parents, you should still be concerned with properly socializing her around people so there are no chances that she will ever nip at the postman or snap at a neighbor's child.

A puppy first learns about behavior with dogs from her littermates and dam.

It Takes All Kinds

The key to successful socialization training is to introduce your Boxer to lots of friendly people so that she grows up adoring *all* humans—people of every size, shape, age, and race. In particular, you'll want to make sure she is familiar and friendly with children, neighbors, and people in uniform, such as the delivery person or mail person.

Children. Kids are typically drawn to puppies like magnets, so if you live in a neighborhood with children, just taking a walk every day will provide the exposure your puppy needs to this group. Lots of pats from children of all ages are just what your Boxer needs to reaffirm her natural love of little humans. If you don't live in a neighborhood with children, consider taking her to a park that is frequented by

children. Or invite a friend with children over from time to time for some supervised play with her.

Neighbors. Introducing your Boxer to your neighbors in a controlled and pleasant manner has a twofold benefit. One is that she will be able to meet more types of people, and two is that your neighbors will see how affable she is. At best, they will love your dog, too; at worst, they will at least understand that she is not dangerous and that you are a responsible owner.

People in uniform. The importance of teaching your Boxer to respect and like people in uniform lies in the fact that if she *doesn't* like these folks, you're likely to have your mail held and your packages go undelivered. And for good reason. The statistics of postal workers being bitten by

Make sure that your Boxer is introduced to many different types of people so that she grows up to be a well-socialized dog.

dog. Praise her! As she becomes less fearful and more trusting of new people, you can decrease the distance at which the person is tossing the food, until the individual is close enough to feed the tidbit by hand.

If someone comes into your home, you can have the Boxer approach the person on her own terms. Have your friend sit in a chair or on the floor, with his or her head turned slightly away from the dog and avoiding eye contact. Yawning once or twice can also help to calm a nervous dog, according to some behaviorists. When the dog looks to be a little curious, have the friend gently (no big motions) toss the treat in the direction of the dog. Gradually let the Boxer come to the person.

Don't rush socializing a shy Boxer or push them too fast. It may take days, weeks, or even months of work for a very frightened Boxer to really begin to trust all humans. However, if you keep up this exercise and don't push her "comfort zone" too much each time, you will begin to see gradual and even immediate improvement.

Also, be careful *not* to reward bad behavior either directly (with a treat) or indirectly by giving the dog verbal reassurances. As mentioned earlier, rewarding the dog in any way when she acts frightened or growls will inadvertently reward her for her poor behavior.

Hint: Since you are using treats as the reward in this exercise, your Boxer may be more amenable to strangers with food if this exercise is done *before* the puppy or adult has had a meal and is just a bit on the hungry side . . .

dogs along their routes is staggering. So, be sure to do your part and introduce your Boxer at an early age to *every* delivery person who comes on a regular or even frequent basis. Your delivery person will greatly appreciate your efforts.

The Shy Boxer

If your Boxer is a bit fearful of strangers at first, have people stand a little farther back, to where she is no longer worried and will stay in a *sit.* Make sure the "stranger" avoids direct eye contact with her, which she may take as a direct threat. Then have the person toss a tidbit to your

Home Schooling

How to Meet and Greet People

Puppies, and Boxers in general, tend to jump up on those they love. So, the first step in socializing your Boxer is to make sure she meets and greets strangers in a somewhat civilized manner. The perfect way to do this is to put your puppy or adult in a *sit* (see Teaching the Sit, page 66). You can work on this skill while simultaneously working on your Boxer's socialization skills.

- When you are coming up to a stranger, put your Boxer in a sit. Then, invite the person to give her a yummy tidbit, which of course you are carrying in your pocket or a fanny pack. The key to this whole exercise is to teach her that an extended hand from *anyone* is a good thing!
- If the treat goes over well, encourage the person to pet your puppy or adult, if they are willing and your Boxer is eager for some attention. Keep in mind that hardly any person can resist patting a cute puppy; however, there may be many folks who are a bit apprehensive when they encounter a full-grown Boxer. Don't force the issue. Respect the person's apprehensions but *do* continue to put your Boxer into a *sit*

when the person approaches, and reward your puppy or dog for sitting quietly.

As you continue to introduce people to your Boxer while you're on your daily walks, you will find that she may no longer need to be reminded to sit every time a stranger approaches, and may start sitting automatically in anticipation of a treat and some attention.

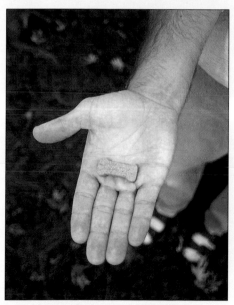

Friendship can be just a treat away!

Puppies and adult Boxers need to be socialized with people of all ages, races, and sizes—kids included!

Boxer Byte: Most Boxers will be enthusiastic about meeting new people and the hardest part in socializing your Boxer will most likely be controlling her and preventing her from jumping up to get more attention. If she is fearful, however, or perhaps a bit aggressive, you might find that she will growl or snarl at someone.

If this happens, do not reward her with a treat. Do not reassure her with hugs and kisses or say, "It's O.K. He's a nice man." By doing this, you will be telling your Boxer that it is O.K. to behave in this manner. If she is frightened by the person, see the tips for shy Boxers (page 40). If, however, she is behaving aggressively toward people, you should immediately begin working with an animal behaviorist for help. Don't wait, the problem will only get worse.

Adopted Adults and People Socialization

If you've adopted an adult Boxer from a breed rescue or shelter, and she has been temperament-tested sufficiently, the people there will know your dog's likes and dislikes, as well as her level of socialization. If she is very friendly with people, keep up the good work! Continue to reinforce these good behaviors.

However, if your Boxer is fearful of people—or of specific groups of people, such as children, people with baseball caps, men, etc.—make sure to work on this in a positive way (see The Shy Boxer, page 40). Many adopted Boxers simply need time and patience before they begin to trust humans again. Be sure to give them this adjustment period.

A Boxer that is territorially aggressive toward strangers (protective of you, your home, yard, etc.) or spontaneously aggressive toward people may be exceptionally dangerous. You should seek out qualified professional help (see Where to Get Help, page 96).

Socializing Your Puppy with Other Dogs

Though you may consider it a "given" that your Boxer puppy *knows* she is a dog and therefore will automatically get along with other dogs, this isn't always the case. Puppies that are separated from their mothers and littermates at an early age—either because of the death of the mother or because the breeder sold the puppies prematurely—have been shown in studies to be a bit confused about who they are and act inappropriately. Fortunately, renewed contact with other canines at an early age seems to help correct some of this behavior, but if the pup goes too long without dog-dog interactions, she may forever be fearful, mistrustful, or aggressive toward other dogs.

Puppy Kindergarten

Therefore, it is important that you keep your Boxer puppy in a social mode with other dogs. An excellent way to do this with a puppy is to enroll in a puppy kindergarten or preschool class. In these classes, a puppy social hour is part of the class. Classes are offered for puppies as young as ten weeks and up to six months old. With leashes off and owners on the sidelines, the puppies are allowed to mix, mingle, and frolic. The class trainer is usually in the middle of the puppies, keeping an eye out for any bully behavior, but in general, allowing the pups to play and learn that "If I play roughly, no one will want to play with me," and other valuable lessons.

Age to Begin Classes

In some areas of the country, certain diseases are so prevalent that it is dangerous to allow your puppy to mix with other puppies until she has received her complete series of puppy vaccinations. This may mean that you cannot begin your puppy classes until your Boxer is 16 weeks old or so.

If this is case, you can still include doggie social time in your Boxer's schedule. You'll just need to know your neighborhood dogs and dog-owning friends. A friendly, adult dog that is fully vaccinated can be a great playmate and teacher for your puppy. Just be sure, however, that the dog is indeed friendly and very tolerant of puppy antics. A bad experience with a dog, such as an attack that sends your puppy screaming for help under your

Well-socialized Boxers know how to have fun!

Take your dog on walks to introduce her to other friendly dogs and neighbors.

legs, can cause your puppy to be fearful of other dogs, even as an adult. Keep things positive, keep things in control, and keep things safe for your puppy. If you follow these rules, your Boxer should be able to continue the rules of canines and grow into a sociable dog.

If your Boxer shows signs of being aggressive toward other dogs, you should begin work immediately to correct the problem. There are some tips included in this book (see Dog-dog Aggression, page 92), but with any form of aggression, it is advisable to seek the help and advice of a professional trainer or animal behaviorist.

Note: If your Boxer puppy is the second dog in your family, be sure to never leave the puppy alone with the adult dog. Many adult dogs are fairly tolerant of puppies, but some dogs are not. Initially, you'll want to supervise their time together and make sure the adult dog accepts the puppy as a member of the family.

Socializing Your Adult Dog with Other Dogs

Though your Boxer's attitude may be somewhat set as to how she views other canines, if you've adopted a sociable Boxer, she will benefit mentally and physically from playing with other dogs. As with a puppy, it is important to screen your Boxer's playmates and make sure they are healthy and not bullies. Always supervise her play just to make sure no one accidently gets hurt. If you frequent a dog park where the dogs are allowed to play off leash in a fenced-in area, don't assume that all dogs are friendly. Get to know the folks who frequent the park and meet their dogs before you bring your Boxer out to play.

If you're the one with the bully (see Dog-dog Aggression, page 92), it would be advisable to work on control exercises, such as putting the dog in a *sit* (see Sit, page 65) when on walks to prevent lunging, or even a *down* (see Down, page 74) for more control. Keep in mind that animal behaviorists feel that dog-dog aggression is perhaps one of the most treatable forms of aggression and that if you are willing to work with your dog, you can make inroads into better behavior.

6 *Habituation*

We often feel that the sights and sounds of our home, neighborhood, and lifestyles are something that our canine companions will readily adapt to and take in stride. We see this happen every day with puppies. Naturally inquisitive, Boxer puppies often will "check out" a new sound or thing. They'll listen, look, and, if nothing happened (and you don't appear to be worried or frightened), they will most likely ignore the "event" the next time it occurs.

For example, the first time your Boxer puppy hears the sound of the dishwasher, he will most likely run over to see what's happening. After thoroughly checking out the situation and determining there is no danger, the next time you turn on the dishwasher he will most likely ignore the event, or at least not be alarmed by it.

This process of learning everyday life events is called *habituation*. And most often, as mentioned in the above example, everything goes smoothly. There are some everyday events, however, that you'll want to practice to make sure they become an easy part of your Boxer's life.

When Something Is Scary

On occasion, things don't go well and your Boxer may show a fearful response to something. It is particularly important during these inappropriate responses to know how to respond so that he will not be frightened in the future.

The biggest mistake you can make when your Boxer is frightened by something, such as a siren, a flapping awning, or a thunderstorm, is to do what we humans are genetically programmed to do: comfort him. Resist the urge to hold him, pet him, or otherwise try to reassure him by saying, *"It's all right."* Why is this a mistake? (It works for kids!) For the same reason it is a mistake to comfort a frightened dog when he growls at a stranger: Because though we see ourselves as comforting the dog, the Boxer sees this attention as a reward for his behavior. In other words, instead of taking action to *decrease* the frightened behavior, we have actually rewarded the dog for his behavior and have begun the cycle of positive reinforcement—but for the *wrong* behavior. Oops.

So, what should you do? First, if something unsettles your Boxer initially, don't make a big deal about it. A fearful, timid, or even startled response can be quite normal when the "something" or event is big and noisy, or something he has never heard or seen before. If you remain calm and settled, he will look to you and take in your response. The next time he is exposed to the scary noise or thing (i.e., a garbage truck), you will most likely find him a bit bolder. However, if you tense up in anticipation of his freaking out over a sight or sound, he will read your anticipation and it is almost *guaranteed* that he will respond exactly as you don't want him to.

So, how do you habituate a dog that has already shown that he has some apprehensions about something? There are four ways to work with this situation, and depending on your Boxer and the particular circumstances, one method may work better than another.

If your Boxer is unsure of something, she will look to you for direction. Your response is important.

The Power of Positive Rewards

It is important to reward your Boxer when he does behave appropriately. For example, if he is apprehensive about the fire trucks that roar out of your neighborhood fire station, try to set him up for success and reward him when he behaves calmly. In other words, if you hear sirens, don't rush your dog out to the curb and force him to be close to the very thing that he fears. Instead, when you hear sirens outside, and your Boxer happens to be behaving normally (no fear), put him in a *sit* and reward him with a treat. You're distracting the dog a bit by giving him a command, but this is O.K. As he becomes more used to the sound in the home, you can gradually take him outside but far away from the sound, and reward as noted above. Basically, the more opportunities you have to reward him for good behavior, the more likely he is to overcome his phobias.

Desensitizing

Another method of allaying fears and phobias involves desensitizing the dog. For example, if your Boxer is deathly afraid of thunderstorms, some animal behaviorists have had success with playing thunderstorm tapes at low levels in the home regularly when there aren't any storms. In this way, the dog becomes accustomed to the sound of the storms and realizes that nothing bad happens to him. Positive reinforcement comes into play because when the dog doesn't pace, whine, bark, drool profusely, or pant, something very good will happen—a treat. Desensitizing works in the same basic way as positive rewards except that desensitizing provides many more exposures to the feared event—in this case, a thunderstorm—and subsequently, many more opportunities to catch the dog behaving appropriately and to reward him.

Removing the Stimulus

Sure, you can spend weeks and months working to have your Boxer overcome certain fears, but in some cases, it's much simpler to remove the cause of the fear. For example, with a dog who is deathly afraid of helium balloons the easiest way to solve the problem is to take the offending balloons out of your Boxer's sight and into another room.

Adapting the Stimulus

Sometimes you can't remove something that is causing your Boxer to behave inappropriately, but you can change the "thing" so that it no longer causes a problem. For example, some adopted Boxers have never seen a large, plate glass window or a screen and will literally try to barge right through them. Unfortunately, this can be quite dangerous.

In the adapting method, the situation is resolved by placing a piece of duct tape (or painter's tape that can be removed later) diagonally across the screen or window. The placement of the tape allows the dog to "see" the screen or glass and

will discourage the dog from trying to jump through the window or door. With time, you should be able to remove the tape and your Boxer will still respect your screens and sliding doors.

The tape across this large window makes it easier for the dogs to see. The same technique can be used to teach a dog not to charge through window screens.

Home Schooling

Everyday Life Habits to Work On

When you bring your Boxer puppy home, he will most likely be quite congenial with everything you want to do with him. The trick is to *keep* him this way! The following are some of the daily living skills your Boxer will need to learn to accept, but that many owners forget to work on. If you wait until you *need* to do these things, you will most likely find yourself in a losing battle with a full-grown Boxer, so start early and keep at it!

Toenail Clipping

■ When your puppy is very little, you can use a cat claw clipper or a small dog clipper to trim his toenails. Take only a tiny piece off when you clip,

Practicing toenail clipping as a puppy will mold an adult dog that is tolerant.

being careful not to "quick" him, or cut the nail too short, which will make the nail bleed.

■ Practice even if he doesn't need it. Make it a habit to handle your puppy's paws every day and even pretend to clip his nails by touching the clipper to his nails.

■ Reward good Boxers with a treat for every toenail. You can gradually fade the treats to every paw, and then after clipping all four paws' nails as he becomes used to the procedure.

■ Distract him. Have another person rub his ears or belly to help distract him and help to make the toenail clipping experience a pleasant one.

■ Older dogs: If you have an adult Boxer that doesn't like his toenails clipped, begin slowly. Clip one toenail, reward him, and let him be. Try for a toenail a day.

■ Practice and use the *stand-stay* or *down-stay*. (See Stay pages 67–69.) Wriggly older dogs will do well during toenail clipping if they are solid on these commands.

Teeth Care

■ With your puppy in your lap, use a finger brush with a little dab of dog toothpaste—*never* use human toothpaste—and rub your puppy's teeth.

■ When he accepts this, you can move to a toothbrush. Remember, he will have a natural tendency while he is teething to try to chew the brush.

Have patience!

■ Adult dogs can be taught to have their teeth brushed, too. With apprehensive dogs, take baby steps. Use a finger brush to begin with and work on his teeth for only a few seconds, rewarding good behavior with a treat.

■ Teaching the *sit-stay* (see Sit, page 65) can help immensely with dental care!

Grooming

■ Most Boxers enjoy being brushed, particularly if you begin when they are puppies.

■ Try to make brushing a daily part of your puppy's care regime—not because he necessarily needs it, but because it will get him used to it.

Baths

■ As with brushing and toenail clipping, your Boxer may not need baths on such a regular basis, but if you don't get him used to water and enjoying his baths, you could find yourself struggling with 60 pounds (27 kg) of muscle that *doesn't* want to get wet. So if possible, rinse your Boxer every two weeks.

■ Make bathtime enjoyable. Use warm water and bathe him outside only if the temperature is warm. When bathing inside in the tub, make sure you have a towel on the bottom of it so that he won't slip.

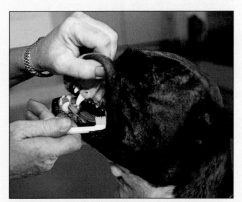

Dental hygiene is important, and only practice will develop a dog's tolerance for a good brushing.

■ Older dogs can learn, too. If you have an adult dog that hasn't had a bath, or is very resistant to the idea, start slowly. Put just a little water in the tub and try to entice him in with a toy, or step in the tub yourself and see if he'll join you. If this fails, put his back legs in first and then coax the rest of his body into the tub. Don't make him stay in too long the first time and reward him for good behavior with a treat. Gradually increase the time he spends in the tub until you can actually give him a bath.

■ Work on his *stand-stay* (see Stand, page 77). If he is solid in his commands, he will be more likely to tolerate a bath. You can then work on actually helping him to enjoy them . . .

The Adult Boxer

Many times a rescued or adopted adult Boxer may need more work in the habituation department than a young puppy. Often, they have led a rather dismal life, relegated to the backyard with minimal indoor time. If he comes from such a background, you should expect to have to show him the "ropes" at home, in the yard, and around the neighborhood.

Often, the newly rescued Boxer will tag along behind you wherever you go in the home, which is actually a great way to habituate your dog to your lifestyle and home. Your fearless reactions to the sights and sounds of your house will be picked up by your Boxer. You can expect to see a few startled expressions as he encounters new experiences. Common "new" experiences can include learning to negotiate slick floors, not being startled by the sound of kitchen appliances (i.e., dishwashers, ice makers, blenders), and figuring out how to climb stairs one step at a time instead of trying to jump them all at once.

You'll find that adult Boxers are ready learners, and with patience, practice, and praise, your adult Boxer will begin settling into your home within a matter of days. Those adopted dogs that have had the benefit of a loving family and many good experiences will often walk into your home, survey the situation briefly, and then begin acting as if they've lived with you all their lives.

The key to habituating the adult Boxer is to anticipate that there will be many new experiences for him. Work steadfastly at establishing his trust in you, and introducing him gradually and gently to the sights and sounds of your home, yard, and neighborhood.

Adult dogs can learn virtually *anything* given time, practice, and patience.

Home Schooling

Teaching Your Boxer the Ropes

If you spend some time introducing your Boxer to your home, yard, neighborhood, and lifestyle activities in a positive way, he will likely settle into your family with no great problems. The best way to do this is to include him as a member of the family from day one.

- Take your Boxer everywhere you can in the car. Try to associate car trips with something more than a visit to the veterinarian's office! Maybe a frolic in the local dog park or a lick from an ice cream cone?
- Carsickness is often a nervous response to travel, so the more trips you make, typically the less nervous your Boxer will become over time. Always use a crate and make sure he is *never* left in a hot car.
- Carry treats with you so you can reward him for good responses no matter where you are. As your puppy or dog becomes more used to the sights and sounds in your neighborhood, you won't need to treat as much, but lots of praise and hands-on attention are always great rewards.
- If you have any particular lifestyle situations that you want to include your Boxer in, such as boating or visiting the beach, make sure you begin including him at a young age and keep things very positive!
- Don't rush him. Recognize when he is experiencing genuine fear, and work with him in a patient, positive manner.
- In severe cases of phobias, consider consulting a certified animal behaviorist or a veterinary animal behaviorist for advice (see Where to Get Help, page 96).

Car travel is something your Boxer will need to become accustomed to so that you can take him everywhere.

7 Beginning Command Training

Now that you are working with your puppy or adult Boxer in the areas of socialization, habituation, and of course, house-training, she is well on her way to becoming a well-adjusted companion. However, if you are like most pet owners,

The well-trained Boxer is a joy to live and work with.

having a semblance of control with your dog is also important, as it should be. There is nothing more well loved than the dog that is well adjusted and well mannered, and not just at home, but everywhere you go.

To achieve this "ideal" Boxer, there is some time and labor involved; however, training her is fun! Don't think of it as a chore, because it's not. If you've chosen the Boxer as your pet and companion, most likely it is because you were attracted to this breed's deep sense of devotion and the simple joy that comes from being around her. Training your dog on a regular basis gives you just one more opportunity to do something constructive and fun with her. If you approach training with the same enthusiasm and joy that she approaches everyday living, you *will* have fun and you *will* have great success.

Equipment Essentials

Getting started with your Boxer's training requires only a few basic purchases. The following is a list of items that you will want to purchase for your Boxer and tips on selecting the best products for your dog.

The Collar

Flat buckle collars. Whether you own a puppy or an adult, your Boxer will need a good, solid flat buckle collar. If you begin training her as a puppy, this may be the only collar you will need for everyday use as well as training. Try to avoid adjustable collars, if possible, because the loop of extra collar length can easily get caught on a branch, nail, or another dog's tooth and quickly strangle her. Boxers tend to get their collars caught on things a bit more often than other dogs, so be sure to take extra precautions that the collar is flat around the dog's neck, not too tight, of course, but also with no extra slack in it that can get caught or hung up on something.

Martingale collars. These are another collar option, but only for training. These collars are fashioned after the sighthound collars, which offer a broad width of collar with loops on either side through which another length of nylon runs. The collar relaxes and tightens as the dog pulls. It is broad, so that it does not choke the dog if she pulls very hard. It does tighten enough, however, that if she attempts to perform an escape move out of her collar, it simply can't be done.

   If you use this type of collar for training, another benefit is that you can put it on in addition to your Boxer's regular collar. The significance of a "special" collar used only for training is not lost on your Boxer. She will quickly recognize that the collar is linked to a training session, which of course is lots of fun. As she progresses in her training, the significance of the special collar may also mean "It's time to listen!"

Flat buckle collar: Leave two fingers of space between the collar and the dog's neck.

Expandable collar with snap closure.

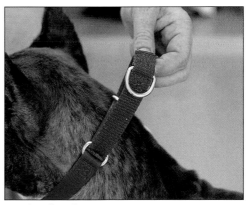
Martingale collar.

Harnesses. Some owners prefer to use harnesses rather than collars on their dogs. The benefit of a harness is that pressure is never put on the dog's neck. (Veterinary chiropractors appreciate this!) If the puppy is trained at an early age not to pull, control is not an issue either, but there are some disadvantages to using a harness.

If you haven't schooled your puppy or adult, be forewarned that a harness actually allows her to pull harder and more efficiently than with a collar. (In weight-pulling competitions, guess what the dogs wear? Right, a harness.) Another potential downside to the harness, particularly if it is worn all the time, is that unless the harness is made of a nice, smooth leather, it may rub your Boxer's coat and skin in some areas. Cost is also a consideration, if you have a puppy, because you will need to buy several harnesses before your Boxer has reached her full size. And finally, a harness provides more opportunities for her to get snagged on something. Granted, if the dog's harness gets

---

Boxer Byte: Some Boxer owners choose to put collars on their dogs only when they are with them because they fear that the opportunities for the dog to get caught and strangle herself are too great. This is true when a Boxer is in her crate; they are known to catch their collars in their crates, strangle, and die. However, leaving your Boxer without a collar at any other time is not a good idea for the following reasons:

■ A dog that bolts out the door or jumps the fence will have no visible identification. Unless someone looks for a tattoo or scans for a microchip, these alternate forms of identification may never be discovered. Both tattoo and microchip registries strongly recommend that the dog wear a tag that states, "I am tattooed," or "I am microchipped" along with the 800-number of the registry.

■ Collars and tags are often seen as a sign that the dog is a pet, and therefore friendly. A dog without a collar and perhaps one that has had some fun in the dirt is often seen as a stray and potentially dangerous, possibly frightening any would-be rescuers from touching the dog.

■ A loose dog that isn't wearing a collar is difficult to catch.

The choice of whether to keep a collar on your Boxer or not is ultimately up to you; however, with supervision and some common sense, the benefits of having your Boxer wear a collar most always outweigh the decision to go collarless. (Just ask Boxer Rescue or your local humane society!)

Harnesses are used for training Schutzhund to avoid neck injuries.

method is proving much more gentle and equally as effective—the head halter.

The Head Halter

The head halter is a relatively new concept in training that may initially look cruel, but is actually a very gentle way for the owner to gain quick control over the dog, particularly with dogs that want to drag their owners down the street. Once you have control, you have the dog's attention. With a dog's attention, she is ready to learn.

The head halter is not to be confused with a muzzle. It is a strap that crosses over the dog's muzzle and loops behind

Head halters are made for brachycephalic breeds, too.

caught on a branch, she won't strangle, as she would with a snagged collar; however, if she is caught and panics, and you're not there when this happens, she can injure herself struggling and possibly even overheat or die.

Heavy artillery. If you own an adult dog that is already mature in size and strength but has had little or no training, you may find that a flat buckle collar or a martingale is not very effective in your initial training efforts. Though some trainers may suggest nylon or metal choke chains (what is called "pop and praise" training), or even a prong collar, in which the prongs pinch the Boxer's neck when she strains against it, an emerging to form a halter. The lead is snapped to a ring that is under the dog's chin.

The head halter works in a similar manner as a horse's halter: Where the head goes, the body will follow. Submissive and complacent dogs rarely put up a fuss about the head halter; however, more dominant dogs may struggle to take it off and try their best to convince you that you are being cruel. You are not! And, there are head halters designed specifically for brachycephalic breeds, such as the Boxer.

For more information on using a head halter, see Useful Addresses and Literature, page 134.

The Leash

In addition to a collar, you will also need to purchase a training leash. For puppies, make sure you purchase the lightest, thinnest leash you can, approximately 6 feet (1.8 m) in length. Yes, you will need to purchase a much sturdier leash when your pup is a bit bigger; however, a large leash now would mean your precious puppy's head would be constantly smacked with a big heavy buckle. So invest in a lightweight leash initially, and then purchase a heavier leash when your puppy is a bit bigger.

If you own an adult Boxer, you can purchase whatever leash you'd like. If your dog pulls a lot, you may consider a leather leash or one made of a cotton web fabric that won't chafe your hands. Nylon is very sturdy, but it can be tough to hold with an untrained and boisterous Boxer. Avoid purchasing any chain link leashes; these products are difficult to hold, cumbersome, and they portray the wrong image for both you and your dog.

Reinforcements

We've talked about positive reinforcements briefly in a previous chapter (see Positive Reinforcement, page 16), but now is the time to think about what type of reinforcement is easiest for you to work with and to which your Boxer responds well.

Food

Used as rewards and lures, food treats are probably the most popular form of reinforcement being used nationwide in training schools. "Treating" a dog is one way to promote positive, gentle training. Food has many benefits as a training tool. It's easy to lure a dog into a position with

> **Boxer Byte:** When using food as lures and rewards, be sure to use foods that are healthy. You want to use treats that are "special," in other words, food that is not given as a staple in their diet, but steer clear of prepackaged treats that are heavy in salt, sugar, and fats. Not only are these unhealthy, but they can cause gastrointestinal problems for your Boxer. If you're unsure if a particular product is healthy for your Boxer, be sure to consult your veterinarian.

food for such commands as *"Sit,"* and *"Down,"* and for various tricks. If used before meals when the dog is hungry, the Boxer is usually motivated to earn its treats. A third benefit, and one of particular interest to owners of deaf Boxers, is that using the treat to position the dog into the command allows the other hand to be free to give the dog a hand signal.

A drawback to the food reward system is that it's simply not a motivator for some Boxers. In particular, dogs that are a bit uncomfortable or uneasy in their surroundings may refuse food. On the other hand, there are some dogs that will do anything for a treat, and when rewarded frequently, gain weight. This can be countered, however, by figuring the food rewards into your puppy's or adult dog's total daily food allowances.

Praise

Boxers can never get too much lovin', and that includes verbal and physical praise. Dogs immediately recognize happiness in our voices, and they also thoroughly enjoy being touched, rubbed, and patted. The effectiveness of praise has been well documented, and is something that should be used when training your Boxer. Verbal and physical praise can be used in conjunction with another reward system such as a treat or toy, or on its own. The advantages to using praise also include that it can be "faded" successfully. In other words, it is easy to transition from praising your dog verbally and physically every time she sits on command, to praising your dog verbally every time and physically every so often, to finally prais-

Treats should be healthy and broken into small pieces so that your Boxer gets just a tidbit at a time.

ing your dog only at the end of a series of successful commands. A drawback to using praise alone in your training is that there is no way to "lure" your dog into position for certain commands.

There's no substitute for warm verbal and physical praise.

57

Home Schooling

The "Five Ws" of Training

To make the most of your training sessions with your Boxer, there are a few basics of training that can make your job *much* simpler. The "Five Ws" of training are as follows.

Who

The "who" of training is, of course, you and your Boxer. It is important that you are in a good mood during the training. If you are having a bad day and are running on a short fuse, this is *not* the time to attempt to work on training your dog. She will read you like a book and attempt to "please" you (i.e., make you happy), but not necessarily by learning and obeying your commands. So make sure that you are as enthusiastic as she is going into your training sessions. Remember: Patience really is a virtue when it comes to training.

What

Proper training equipment for both handler and Boxer is important. You should be sure to wear athletic shoes for good grip and traction. Loose floppy shoes are difficult to move well in and are also a distraction to a playful Boxer—a new chew toy! The training essentials for your dog have

already been covered in this chapter but include a good collar, leash, and treats or other rewards.

Where

Aside from your weekly group training sessions with a trainer, your daily sessions should be in areas with very few distractions so that your Boxer can really focus on you. In the beginning, you're really trying to maximize the potential for her to do the right thing: You're not trying to test her at this point. So don't try to teach her the *sit* in the kitchen if someone is cooking dinner on the stove, or in the backyard if you have children or other pets running around. Try to keep your daily sessions in a quiet place with few distractions. As she becomes more proficient in her command work, then you will want to begin working in areas with more and more distractions.

When

When you are just starting out training your Boxer, whether you own an adult or a puppy, she will need many successful repetitions of a task to learn the behavior you want her to perform. What this means is that the more mini-sessions you can have throughout the day and evening, the faster she will learn because you are constantly reinforcing her correct response to the command. If you don't have the benefit of being home all day to work off and on with your Boxer, the next best method is to schedule two or three short sessions of five minutes or so, spread out in a day.

Shorter training sessions also help to keep her from becoming bored and adding new twists to the exercises being taught. A Boxer, as mentioned earlier, likes to keep life interesting and this extends to her training. Keep the training sessions interesting and playful, and always stop before she tires either mentally or physically. Timing is important!

Why

The importance of a well-trained Boxer has already been discussed previously in this chapter, but in summary, it is important to train her to be a good canine for several reasons:

■ A well-behaved dog is a joy to live with.
■ A well-trained dog is less of a liability in this lawsuit-happy world.
■ Every minute you put into training your dog deepens the bond you have with her—and isn't that what dog ownership is all about?

Never take a bad day out on your Boxer.

Toys

Some Boxers are crazy about balls. If you own a ball-crazed Boxer, you may very well want to use a tennis ball on a rope for your reward system. Padded, sausage-like tug toys on a rope can also be used very successfully in training. Though luring a dog into position with a toy can be cumbersome, working with the toy as a reward can be very successful.

When using the toy as a reward, keep the toy out of sight or in your right hand, depending on the exercise you are working on. When the dog completes the command or exercise, reward her by allowing her to grab and play with the toy. Balls and toys on a rope work well because you can hold one end of the toy at all times. When the reward/play is over, you can then give the *out* command (see Out, page 79), and take back the toy.

Clicker Training

This form of training is extremely popular and has a very loyal and growing following of trainers, animal behaviorists, and owners. Clicker training conditions the dog to accept a "click" from a clicker (we used to call them "crickets" as kids) as a verbal reward and a promise of a treat. Initially, the treat comes with every click; this is how the dog learns to associate a click with a treat. Then the treats are faded so that the dog still gets treated when she has received clicks, but the treat may not come until the dog has received several clicks.

The main advantages to clicker training are in the method's precision, and the ability to reward the dog at a distance by sound. The precision of a click is much more exact than trying to say *"Good, girl!"* or treating a dog. With verbal praise, the timing is approximate to when the dog performs the task. With treats, the dog typically doesn't get rewarded until after she has performed the task. With the clicker, the dog knows she is being rewarded *while* she is performing the task.

As for distance training, clicker training works when your dog is out of reach. For example, if you are training your dog to jump though a hoop, with clicker training you can now "click" and thereby reward your dog while she is airborne going through the hoop!

The only real disadvantage to this system is that the owner needs to have a certain level of coordination to be able to handle the dog, treats, and clicker. Additionally, if an owner is not familiar with this form of training, it is helpful to find a trainer who is and work with him or her for a while. To learn more about clicker training, see Useful Addresses and Literature, page 134.

Selecting a Trainer and Training School

Now that you know some of the basic ways in which to train your Boxer, you should begin your search for a good training school and trainer. Though this book will give you many training tips and strategies, it is really meant as a guide to get you started in the right direction and to understand, especially if your trainer doesn't, how and why the Boxer is a bit different to train than other breeds. In short, nothing beats hands-on training with an experienced trainer and the many benefits that only a group class can offer you and your dog.

So how do you find a training class? One of the best ways is to simply ask. Ask your veterinarian what school he or she recommends. Ask the local humane society for a recommendation. If you're fortunate enough to live in the same area as your breeder, be sure to ask him or her for a recommendation. Do you have any neighbors who have well-trained dogs that you admire? Ask them where they went for training.

You'll quickly find that one or two training clubs are mentioned frequently. When you're at this point, call the school and talk to them about the class, what types of things are taught (it should be a mixture of command work along with socialization—for puppies—and troubleshooting typical problem behaviors), and what type of experience and accreditations or certifications the trainer has. If this goes well, your next step is to arrange to visit a class—without your Boxer—while it is in session.

When you're at the school, you'll want to watch for several things.

■ Is the training facility clean? When training young puppies it is critical that the floors are kept clean to prevent infection. Remember that puppies that begin training are usually in the middle of their vaccination series, and there-

fore are still susceptible to a variety of diseases. Even if you are training an adult dog, cleanliness counts. Health dangers still lurk in dirty surroundings.

■ What is the tone of the class? Training should be fun. If the trainer is heavy-handed and not *fun* you'll pick this up quickly by the way the students in the class are participating.

■ Does the trainer inspire you? A great trainer combines skill, experience, and enthusiasm and freely shares all of this with his or her students. A trainer who is lacking in any or all of these areas is not a good choice.

Hint: If you're not comfortable with the trainer, no matter how awesome his or her reputation, you're not going to listen as well or benefit much from the trainer's experience.

■ Does the trainer teach using the tools and reinforcements you want to use? If you're interested in clicker training, make sure you find a trainer comfortable with this method of training. If you'd like to work with a head halter, make sure the trainer is skilled in training with this tool.

■ Do you see any slip or choke collars? If you are watching a puppy class and you see choke collars being used, find another class. Young puppies as a general rule never need this type of correction. If you're watching an adult training class and you see slip collars, you may want to ask the trainer why these collars are being used.

■ Does the trainer like Boxers? As hard as this may be to fathom, there are trainers who will groan and roll their eyes if they hear someone wants to train a Boxer. What this tells you is that the trainer is inexperienced working with this breed and you should find another trainer. Someone who has worked with Boxers and is skilled with them will be delighted to have the opportunity to work with such a wonderful creature!

If you like what you see and you enjoy the trainer, then sign up. Many schools fill their early puppy classes in a hurry, so if this happens to be the situation, don't despair. Sign up for the earliest available class and make sure to get your name on the waiting list of any other classes that precede it. Owners often sign up for classes but never attend or drop out quickly. Sometimes this can mean a space may open up. It's worth a try.

If it will be a few weeks before you can get into a class or if your veterinarian does not recommend joining a group class until your puppy is 16 weeks old, due to the health of your puppy or the prevalence of certain deadly diseases in your particular area, this doesn't mean you can take time off until class time! With a young puppy it is important to begin training right away, and with the guidelines in this book, you can already have your puppy responding to quite a few commands within a few weeks.

If you're working with an adult Boxer, the chances are much greater that you will find an open class, but if you can't, there's no reason to wait to train your dog either. Start at home, keep it positive, and have fun, because, isn't F-U-N how you spell "Boxer"?

8 *Five Basic Commands*

You and your Boxer can potentially "get by" knowing very few commands. Depending on your lifestyle and what you expect from him, the basic five commands—*Name, Sit, Stay, Come,* and *Walk nicely*—can be quite sufficient for most pet owners.

What many dog owners discover though, is that they enjoy teaching their dogs new commands and tricks. So whether you read past this chapter to pick up additional home-living skills to teach your Boxer, or if you simply stop with the "favorite five," it is really up to you and your family's needs. Regardless of how far you take your Boxer, teaching a few (or a lot) of commands will help to shape a controllable and fun pet.

Name

A favorite anecdote among dog owners is a story of the dog that *didn't* know his name. Or rather, the dog believed his name to be a certain swear word (for the sake of propriety, the words "darn it" will be substituted). How did this happen? Well, when the dog ran off, the owner would yell, *"Darn it, come here!"* and the dog would. When the dog was jumping up all over the owner with muddy paws, the owner would holler, *"Darn it, sit!"* And the dog would sit. However, the owner was confounded when he would say, *"Patches, sit,"* and the dog wouldn't even look at him. As the yarn goes, the dog thought his name was "Darn it!" and didn't know to respond to "Patches."

As soon as your puppy responds to his name by looking at you, reward him with a little treat.

The owner's constant use of "darn it" as the attention-getting word for the dog became the dog's name, or so the dog thought.

Though this yarn is just that—a yarn—it is not entirely out of the realm of possibility. In order to respond to a command, a dog must first know you mean *him*. Whatever word you use to gain the dog's attention sets the dog up to listen to what is coming next. Most often, this "set-up" word is the dog's name.

Boxer Byte: If you plan on competing in performance events, depending on the type of event, you may want to carefully choose a name. Two-syllable names generally roll easiest off the tongue; however, sometimes names can be so similar in sound to a command that the dog has difficulty differentiating between his name and the word for what you want him to do. "Rover" might confuse the *over* command, "Trey" with *stay*, and "Fletch" with *fetch*.

Of course, if you have your heart set on a certain name or that's the one your Boxer came with, there are ways around everything. First, you can work on teaching your dog hand signals so that there is no confusion between the dog's name and a command. Second, you can simply change the word used for the command. Instead of *"over,"* you might use *"jump"* or *"bar."*

Teaching the Name

Assuming you're going to go the route of using the dog's name as the set up word for his commands, the following is how you go about teaching a young puppy or a newly adopted adult Boxer his name.

1. With a treat in your right hand and your left hand relaxing at your side, say the dog's name.
2. When he responds by looking at you, immediately reward him.
3. Practice this until you are confident he knows his name, then fade the treats so he is rewarded less often with food, but always with praise.

Alternative method.
1. Say his name while taking a treat under the dog's nose and raising it to your chin.
2. Treat him for watching you.

For deaf Boxers.
1. Determine an effective, attention-getting tool, such as a penlight to cross the dog's line of vision, a stomp on the floor (this only works when you're in a home, not outside), or a mild buzz on a pagerlike electronic collar, which works anywhere at any distance once the Boxer learns that the vibration means something yummy is coming from you.
2. When you make eye contact, immediately treat him.
3. Practice frequently.

Whatever method you use, as long as you use it consistently and repeat it many times throughout the day, initially rewarding at every correct response, it will not take long for the dog to quickly learn his name and understand that he must look to you for what's next. What's next, of course, is learning the *sit*.

Sit

If your Boxer learns only *one* command, this is it: the *sit*. The *sit* command comes in handy for so many things in everyday life that it is virtually indispensable.

- If your Boxer tends to want to jump and hug every person on earth, a *sit* command can keep him on the ground.
- When it's feeding time, a *sit* command keeps the dinner bowl from being knocked to the floor.
- A *sit* can be used to keep your Boxer from rushing through open doors ahead of you.
- It can also be used as a "defusing" command. If he is behaving badly or simply is too wound up, you can put him on a *sit,* and then reward him for this "good" behavior.
- A solid *sit* command has also been used more than once to catch a loose Boxer or to break up a dogfight.

So, without anything more said, the *sit* command is very valuable, and who knows how many ways you will be able to use this command. The more you practice it at home and around the neighborhood, the faster and more consistently your Boxer will respond.

Boxer Byte: Many people will automatically begin giving their dogs what is called a release command after the dog has performed a task; however, it is important that the word used to release your dog from a command is the same every time. Many owners choose to use "O.K." or "Yes!" which are both fine choices. The release should be a single word—your Boxer won't focus in on longer phrases—and it should be something that you use naturally when your Boxer has done something great.

As you move the treat over the dog's head, he will naturally sit.

Teaching the Sit

1. With your hand gently holding your dog's collar, say his name.
2. Hold a treat in the palm of your right hand with your fingers wrapped around it.
3. When you have achieved eye contact, begin passing the hand with the treat directly in front of your dog's nose slowly over the top of his head to about the back of the skull while saying the command *"Sit."* Your hand should be so close to the top of your dog's head as to almost brush the hairs. What should happen is that he will follow the treat with his nose and as you move it farther back, he will automatically sit.
4. If you fail to get your Boxer to sit on your first try, don't give up! Try again, making sure not to allow him to back up while the treat is passing over his head. This will force him to tuck in his rear end, rock back, and sit.
5. Once you have him sitting, give him his well-earned treat, enthusiastically give your release word, and give lots of pats and praise!

Hand Signals

Once you have your Boxer sitting without having to pass the food over his head to shape the *sit,* you can begin adding a hand signal.

1. Holding the treat in your right hand, say his name.
2. When you have his attention (which should be immediate now), raise your left hand and, while giving the hand

3 Release, praise, and treat, of course!

4. As your Boxer begins sitting regularly on command, begin fading the verbal cue, saying *"Sit"* only sometimes while giving the hand signal. If your dog doesn't respond immediately, refrain from giving the command again; instead, shape your Boxer into a *sit* with a treat while giving the hand signal.

5. Practice, practice, practice!

Stay

If *sit* is a good command to know, then *sitting* and *staying* are even better! The *stay* command is another very practical command for your Boxer to learn, and it may even save his life someday. The *stay*

The hand for the *stay* signal moves from right to left.

Boxer Byte: A mistake that many new owners make when working their dogs is to repeat commands. This is a no-no because in the operant conditioning training method, which we're using here with rewards, if you repeat the command several times before the dog responds, you're actually teaching your dog to be slow and wait for several commands.

So what do you do if your dog doesn't respond the first time to a command? When he really knows his commands well and doesn't respond, it is often because you don't have his attention. So, make sure you have his attention before giving any commands; you want to set your Boxer up for success, not try to test his learning ability. Then, if you have the dog's attention and he doesn't perform the command, help him. Take him back to square one and lure him into position using a treat. Rebuild his response to the command being careful not to go too fast with him.

---

signal of your choice, say *"Sit."* For hand signals, you may use a touch to the chin, a point to the ground, the American Sign Language symbol for *sit,* or a hand signal that you choose that is specific to a certain performance event. Whatever you chose, make sure you are consistent and make the same hand gesture every time you say *"Sit."*

command comes in handy when clipping his toenails, giving him baths, grooming him, and preventing him from bolting out the front door, as well as preventing a loose Boxer from getting hit by a car.

The *stay* command is a relatively easy task to teach your Boxer; however, it is important to note that you should never "test" your dog off leash on the *stay* command in an unfenced area, just in case the motivators you are using (praise, treats, toys, etc.) aren't quite as motivating as the dog next door or the child walking by with an ice cream cone.

Move a step or two away to test the *sit-stay*.

Teaching the Stay Command

1. Get your dog's attention by saying his name.
2. With him at your left side, put him into a *sit*.
3. Holding the leash in your right hand, say "*Stay*" while, with your left hand, give the hand signal for *stay* directly in front of his nose. The hand signal is generally a flat hand, palm facing toward the dog, fingers pointing toward the ground.
4. Remain in this position for a few seconds, then reward him with a release command and a treat. Gradually increase the length of the stay command. If at any time he tries to move, stand up, or wiggle around, put the dog back into a *sit* and repeat the command "*Stay*."
5. As your Boxer becomes more proficient with the *stay* command, you can increase the amount of time that he must sit next to you by a minute. The next level would be to put him in a *stay* and then slowly walk around him.
6. A more advanced level would be to put your Boxer in a *sit-stay* and walk away from him to the end of the leash, turn, and return to him. If you really want to test the *sit-stay* you can buy a tracking or recall leash (a retractable leash works well for this, too, except that it gives a little pull when you are letting out the leash) and test your Boxer at greater distances and for longer times.
7. Be sure not to push your Boxer too soon. It's better to go a bit slower and make sure he has learned the *sit-stay* than to rush to more advanced levels

of the *stay,* fail (the dog breaks the *stay*), and have to retrace your steps.

To the Test?

Unless you are planning to enter a competitive sport with your dog, it is advisable *never* to try out or test your dog's abilities to follow your commands off leash in an unfenced area. Why? Because without the ability to enforce the command, such as a leash to catch your dog before he runs off, your Boxer's learning is inconsistent.

On the reality side of things: Even if you are sure that your Boxer is steady on his *sit-stay* command, the one time you try this off leash in an open area is the one time it is virtually guaranteed that a squirrel or rabbit will run right under his nose. Now you have a loose dog that is far more motivated by the running critter than the treat in your hand. You also have a Boxer that has learned maybe he doesn't have to do everything you ask him to.

If you are training for Agility, competitive obedience, Schutzhund obedience, or other dog sports, you will eventually need to work with your dog off leash as part of your training and testing, but this work is still performed in protected, fenced-in areas.

The real test of what your dog has learned is, of course, in the emergency situation when you *really* need your dog to *sit, stay,* or *come.* Hopefully, you won't have to be confronted with this type of situation, but if you are—and you've really worked hard with your Boxer—the odds are in your favor that he will indeed listen to you and obey your command willingly.

Come

The *recall* exercise, as it is called in formal obedience, is not only practical, but it may just be what saves your wayward Boxer's life some day. The *come* command is not difficult to teach with either puppies or adults. As with any exercise, this command should not be taught off leash. If you are planning to participate in obedience trials, you will have to recall your dog off leash; however, this exercise should only be practiced off leash if he is very solid in his on-leash *recall,* and you are in a fenced protected area.

There are several exercises that work on teaching the *come* command. The following are a few favorites that involve all family members.

Teaching the Come

1. In a room in the house or in a fenced backyard, have family members sit in a circle.
2. With a lightweight leash on the dog, have one family member hold him gently.
3. Have another family member (only one!) first say the Boxer's name (this is to get his attention), then, *"Come!"*
4. Immediately following the command, the family member should do whatever it takes to entice the Boxer to come running to him or her.
5. When he comes running, do not lunge or grab for the collar (this can start him on a perpetual game of keep-away), but catch the leash. Praise profusely and treat!

The *recall* game should be played in a fenced yard, with the dog dragging a leash.

6. Once the Boxer has received his treat, have another family member call him and continue the exercise.

Note: Be sure not to go too long with this exercise. You want your Boxer joyful and eager to come running to you. Be sure to quit the game while he wants more.

Alternative method. Of course, not everyone has a full family at their disposal to play the *come* game. If you are on your own, however, there are still some fun exercises you can do to help teach your Boxer that "come" does indeed mean *"come."*

1. Give the *come* command whenever you catch your Boxer running toward you. As simple as this sounds, if you are consistent in giving the command—and it should be in a joyful and excited

manner (who would want to come running to a surly owner?)—your Boxer will quickly connect that running to you means good things.
2. Praise your Boxer lavishly for coming and treat, of course!

Note: This manner of teaching the *come* command can work well if your dog knows you have a sack of treats with you, and it's before suppertime.

On-leash Come

Once your Boxer has figured out that *"come"* means to come running, you can work on the exercise in combination with a *sit-stay* while on a leash. The benefit to using the *sit-stay* and a leash for this intermediate level of the *recall* is that you can now work on this exercise in a variety of locations, not just your fenced backyard or a room in your home. The more your Boxer is accustomed to coming when you call him, in all sorts of surroundings, the more likely he will come when you really need him to.

1. Put your Boxer in a *sit-stay* and walk to the end of the leash.
2. Say his name to get his attention.
3. Give the *come* command and start jogging a bit backwards while enthusiastically encouraging him to come running, but being careful not to repeat the *come* command.
4. When he catches up with you, praise him lavishly and give the him some treats.
5. If you are planning to compete in obedience at some point, you will

Boxer Byte: To really put speed and dazzle on your *recall*, Norbert Zawatzki, Director of Training for the German Boxer Club, recommends tossing a ball through your legs and behind you just as your Boxer approaches you. He will come zooming through your legs and snatch up the ball behind you. The tossed ball not only motivates him to run hard on his *recall*, it is also his immediate reward for coming so quickly, and a great way to keep training fun.

Off-leash *recalls* are required in some performance events.

eventually want to add a *sit* in front of you and a *finish to heel* position. This isn't necessary now, however, because you want that unbridled enthusiasm of a Boxer streaking toward you!

6. The *recall* can be performed at increasingly longer distances using a tracking leash or retractable leash.

Involving the Kids

If you have children, training your Boxer to listen to their commands is as important as training him to listen to your commands. As a family dog that likes to be involved in *everything*, if your Boxer listens to your children, group playtimes can become even more fun. Also, children tend to be avid learners when it comes to dog training and will (generally) readily accept your instructions.

First, make sure your Boxer is steady in responding to a command before you

Children should be involved in the puppy's training, too.

71

Precision heeling is only achieved through maintaining the dog's attention and keeping it fun.

attempt to have your children learn to give him the same command. A good first command to teach is the *sit.* Have your child stand next to you, facing your dog, and give your dog the command *"Sit."* (If your child is small, sit down and put your child in your lap.) When the Boxer sits, have your child reward him with a treat. Release the dog *("O.K!")* and then have your child give him the same *sit* command, and reward as soon as he sits.

Tip: If you have young children (5 to 13), you might consider teaching hand signals to them and your Boxer for the commands. A child's high-pitched voice lacks

the authority of an adult, but a hand signal "reads" the same. Also, make sure your children know not to try to "train" the dog while you are not there. They could very quickly confuse the dog or train him to do something you don't want him to!

Walk Nicely

If there's one common complaint about the Boxer, it is that this breed, when not trained, has a fond tendency of dragging his hapless owner on walks. Motivators, such as treats, praise, and balls, can work—but only to a certain point. Why? Because when you are out on a walk, there are generally so many fascinating things that your Boxer just can't wait to explore. You have a treat in your hand? Huh. That's nothing compared to that puppy across the street or the bird that just flew up in that tree or that leaf falling from a bush or—you get the point.

Walking nicely on a leash can be difficult to train for many owners mainly because Boxers have such a great interest in their surroundings coupled with a virtually endless supply of energy; however, there are quite a few training techniques and tools available that can make this job simpler.

Training the Walk Nicely

1. Allow your Boxer to burn off a little energy (if possible) in the backyard with a game of chase or some ball throwing.

2. Attach a 6-foot (1.8-m) leash with a suitable clip (small for little puppies, large is fine for adults).
3. Carry (and make sure your Boxer *knows* you are carrying) a motivator such as treats or a favorite tug toy.
4. Begin walking. If you are planning on competing in obedience at some point, be sure to begin with your *left* foot, leaning into the first step for a body cue. This left step will later signal your dog to move with you as opposed to staying in place, which will be indicated by leading off with your *right* foot.
5. Use your voice and lots of praise, as well as occasional treats to keep your Boxer's attention focused on you.
6. To keep his attention, trying mixing things up. If he goes one way, you go the other. If he lunges ahead, do an about-turn and being walking the other way. If he veers left, turn to the right quickly. If he lags, speed up and encourage him to catch up. Keep changing directions until he realizes he must pay attention or he will be left behind.
7. If you are carrying a tug toy or a ball on a rope, carry this in your right hand (your Boxer is on your left) and swing your right arm so that he catches glimpses of the toy, recommends Zawatzki. Occasionally let your Boxer have the toy and play a short game as a reward. (This works wonders with adult Boxers, too.)

Toys can be used to encourage attention and motivation.

Problem Pullers

If a Boxer is not walked frequently as a puppy, problems can occur when the dog matures or is later adopted as an adult dog. For heavy pullers or adult dogs that just can't seem to pay attention to *you*, look into investing in a head collar (see Head Collars, page 55).

9 *Nine More Commands*

Ready to learn some additional commands for your Boxer? With the basics in Chapter 8, you should be well on your way to having a great house dog, but these additional commands will give you some additional control. Choose those that are most needed for your lifestyle and work on them a few times for short periods throughout the day.

Down

The *down* command is a very useful tool in everyday Boxer life. If you happen to have a Boxer that thinks she is queen of the neighborhood, putting her in a *down* when she attempts to growl or lunge at other dogs on walks can help. Dogs are less likely to growl in this position. Another example of this command's use is as a settling tool. The *down* position can be used to help quiet a Boxer that has a temporary case of the rowdies.

Teaching the Down

1. With your Boxer at your left side (and on leash) put her in a *sit*.
2. Holding a treat in one hand, move the treat from right in front of her nose slowly down to the floor while saying the command *"Down."* She should follow the treat to the floor and wind up lying down.
3. When she is lying down, reward her with the treat.
4. Give her the release word, praise, and pat!
5. Be sure when working with this command that your dog realizes she cannot break the *down* until you give the release command.

Problems with the Down

Sometimes dogs will try to stand from the *sit* to get the treat as it moves to the floor in your hand. If this happens, say *"Ah!"* and put your Boxer back in a *sit*. Once solidly in a *sit*, begin the exercise again.

Another problem that often crops up with the *down* command is that the handler uses this command for an action other than the *down* and confuses the dog. Frequently, people will say *"Get down"* when they want their dogs to hop off a couch. Don't confuse your Boxer! Instead, use the *off* command (see Off, pages 76–77) for those times when you want your Boxer to get off a chair, couch, or bed.

Boxer Byte: As mentioned in the last chapter, if you own a deaf dog, make sure to use a hand signal with the treat lure. The downward movement of your hand holding the treat can be the hand signal for the down. Or, you can give a different hand signal first and then lure with the treat.

Note how this trainer uses a hand signal and a motivator (the tug toy) to teach the *down*.

Use the treat as a lure to move the dog into a *down*.

Teaching the Down-Stay

Once your Boxer has mastered the *down,* you can begin working on the *down-stay.* This is done in much the same way that the *sit-stay* is taught (See Sit, pages 65–67.)

1. Put your Boxer in a *down.*
2. Bend over and give her the *stay* hand signal with your left hand (fingers down, palm toward the front of her nose, and a right-to-left motion).
3. If your Boxer understands the word "stay," walk a few steps away beginning with your *right* foot. Come back to her. If she doesn't know what "stay" means, don't walk away from her; stand still next to her for a few seconds.

4. Release, praise, and treat!
5. As your dog gets steadier in staying with this command, you can walk farther away until you are at the end of the leash. To practice this at an even greater distance, use a recall leash. Eventually, a puppy should be able to *down-stay* for several minutes at a time. (Adult Boxers will be able to *down-stay* for much longer periods.)

Off

This is the command that is used to get your Boxer off the couch, off the bed, or off any other piece of furniture she shouldn't be on. As mentioned above, be sure not to use the word "down" for this command because it only creates confusion.

This Boxer has learned a solid *down-stay.*

Teaching the Off

1. Say your Boxer's name to get her attention.
2. Take her gently by the collar if needed and coax her off the furniture or bed, saying the command *"Off."*
3. Praise her and take her to another room or area.
4. If you'd like, you can add a hand signal (a sweeping motion works well) when you say the command *"Off."*

Use the command *"Off,"* and not *"Get down,"* to avoid confusion.

Stand

Teaching your Boxer to stand *still* on all four feet may seem like an impossibility, particularly if you have a Boxer that prefers to be airborne; however, this simple command is crucial for everyday grooming procedures. It also is a command that your veterinarian will greatly appreciate during yearly examinations! If you are considering competitive obedience or perhaps showing your Boxer in the conformation ring, the *stand* is something you will need to teach her, too.

Teaching the Stand

1. With your Boxer on leash and at your left side, take a couple of steps forward, pull back slightly to halt her and—here's the part that requires a bit of coordination—put your left hand, fingers down, in front of her nose as you say *"Stand."*
2. If your Boxer tries to sit, quickly scoop her up by putting your hand under her abdomen area.

The *stand* is necessary for the show ring and Obedience.

If she tries to sit, scoop her up, and repeat the *"Stand"* command.

Eventually, you will be able to step farther away from your dog in the *stand-stay.*

3. Release her when she is standing still.
4. Praise and treat her.

Teaching the Stand-Stay

The second part of this command is the *stay* portion. To teach this to your dog, follow these steps.

1. In the *stand* position, give your Boxer the *stay* hand signal (a quick right to left, fingers down movement).
2. Holding the leash in your right hand and pulling up just enough to "feel" your Boxer, stay in this position for a few seconds and then release her. Praise and treat!
3. Gradually increase the time you ask your Boxer to stand without moving. (If she moves a foot, say *"Ah!"* and move the foot back into position.)
4. Add distance to the *stand-stay.* Take a few steps away, or walk around your dog.
5. As she progresses, you will eventually be able to walk away from her in varying distances. Be sure to always keep a leash on her so that you can control your dog if she should break her *stand-stay.*

Back

This is a handy little command that often is taught without the owners even knowing they are teaching it. Basically, it is much the same technique that is used when teaching horses to *back,* except that the owner is, of course, not on the Boxer's back! The *back* command can be used whenever your Boxer (or Boxers) are crowding you as you enter a doorway or gated area and you need the dog to back up so you can get in.

Teaching the Back

1. With the dog standing in front of you, simply say the command *"Back"* as you walk slowly into her.
2. She will automatically back up to stay out of your way.
3. Praise her when she backs up.

Stepping into your Boxer and saying *"Back"* is another way to teach your dog to back up.

Alternate method.
1. With your Boxer at your left side, and between you and a wall, say the command *"Back"* as you lean into the wall slightly and back toward her.
2. Your Boxer will back up to get out of your way.
3. Praise and treat her.

Take It and Out

The Boxer's bite is made for holding onto things and not letting go. So if you plan on playing tug with her, or if you are to have any hope of retrieving a wayward shoe from her jaws, you'll need to teach her the *out* command.

Of course, going hand-in-hand with the *out* command is the *take it* command, and the two can be taught simultaneously.

Teaching the Take It

1. Choose a toy that your Boxer really, really wants to take in her mouth and play with. For some dogs this might be a favorite ball or a stuffed dog toy. (Food items, such as meaty bones, should be avoided. Though your Boxer will gladly take it, there could be some issues with resource guarding that could make the "out" part of the exercise unnecessarily difficult.)
2. Standing in front of your Boxer, put her in a *sit*.
3. Hold the toy near her mouth (so she doesn't have to break the *sit* to get it), and say *"Take it!"*

79

4. When she opens her mouth and takes the toy, immediately give her a release command (so she can break the *sit*) and play a little tug with her or let her run around shaking her prize.

5. If you are considering competitive obedience, be sure to include dumbbells as some of the fun toys your Boxer can "take" and play with. (Don't let her play with them unsupervised.) This is a technique commonly seen in Germany that incorporates retrieving items into the assortment of play items. It works! If your Boxer sees the dumbbell as something fun to pick up, you will rarely have a problem with retrieves later.

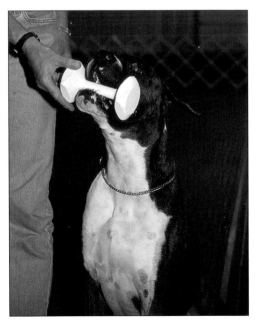

Give the *take it* command when you offer your Boxer something she'd like to hold.

Teaching the Out

If you plan on playing tug with your Boxer, it is very important that she learns the *out* command at a very early age. Some animal behaviorists feel that if a dog is allowed to constantly "win" at tug, she will translate this as meaning that she is dominant over the "tugee." This is a particularly dangerous impression for a dog to have, particularly if she is playing tug with a child who has little opportunity to exercise leadership with the dog. With this in mind, it just makes sense to set the rules early with tug games and make sure that the human sometimes wins. This can be done by commanding the dog to release the tug when *you* want her to, by using the *out* command.

This is easiest to teach a young puppy, but with some patience and practice, adults can also be taught this command.

1. With the dog under control (hand on the collar or dog on leash), say her name and give her the *sit* command. (This gets her attention and alerts her that playtime is over.)
2. Saying the word *"Out,"* grasp the toy or tug with one hand and gently pull it from her mouth.
3. Praise her and give her a treat.

Stubborn Boxers

If the dog won't release the toy, don't resort to any desperate measures! (Some trainers will have you dig a fingernail into the dog's gums or pinch an ear to get them to open their mouths—*don't do this!*) An easy way to get the clenched jaw

If your Boxer doesn't want to give something up, chances are you will be the loser in this game of tug—unless your dog knows the *out* command.

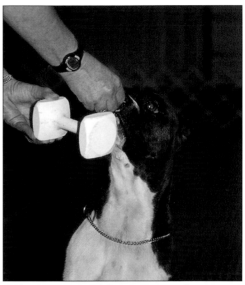

Entice your Boxer with a treat to get her to release an item.

Boxer to open her mouth is to offer her something better, such as a dog cookie or perhaps a favorite bone. Be sure to say the word *"Out"* as she releases the toy for the anticipated treat. Repetition works wonders and your Boxer will quickly learn that releasing the item means a treat.

Leave It

This command is closely related to the *out* command, except you never allow the dog to take the article or item. This command can be practiced frequently on walks when you want your Boxer *not* to pick up something, such as a dead bird.

Teaching the Leave It

1. While walking your Boxer on a leash, keep an eye out for things that she might like to pick up.
2. *Before* she snatches up an item, but when you sense she is heading for it, pull back gently on the leash, say your dog's name (for attention purposes), and say firmly, *"Leave it!"*
3. Praise and treat her as you walk away from the item.

As you repeat this command over days and weeks of walking, you will find that your Boxer will quickly pick up on what *"Leave it"* means, and you will be able to use it in other circumstances, too, such as

81

Pat your chest and say *"Hugs"* to encourage your dog to jump up when *you* want her to.

when she spots a cat across the street and is thinking about dragging you along with her for a good chase.

Kisses/Hugs

Boxers *love* their people and are known for their excited and boisterous hellos. The wild jumping and licking that accompanies the typical Boxer greeting is O.K. in some instances, but if you are easily toppled, tend to wear clothes that you preferred weren't "signed" with muddy paw prints, or if you have guests, you'll want to control this exuberant greeting. The *kisses/hugs* command allows your Boxer to greet you when you want her to and in a more controlled manner.

Teaching the Kisses/Hugs

1. When your dog is leaping in the air, wild with excitement, say her name and put her in a *sit*. (She must be good at the *sit* for you to teach the second part of this exercise.)
2. Now that she is in a *sit,* pat your chest with your hands and say *"Kisses"* or *"Hugs,"* allowing her to slurp and hug you.
3. When you've had enough, and before your Boxer becomes too excited again, put her back in a *sit*.
4. Release and reward with *calm* praise and treats.

Up/Hup

The last command of this chapter that is quite helpful in everyday living is the *up* or *hup* command. Similar to the *back* command (see Back, page 78), the *up/hup* command is often taught without the owner consciously realizing it. The command is useful when asking your Boxer to jump into your car, or onto a steady, solid grooming table.

Teaching the Up/Hup

1. Pat the surface you'd like your dog to jump to and say *"Up"* or *"Hup."* The best surfaces to begin teaching this command to your Boxer are usually those that are low and easy for her to hop up on, and a surface she would *really* like to be on, such as a couch with a dog blanket on it, or perhaps a corner of the bed.
2. When she jumps onto the surface, praise and treat her.

The *hup* or *up* command allows you to tell your dog to jump up on or into something, such as a car.

It's as simple as that! With repetition, your dog will follow this command on virtually any surface and anywhere.

10 *Five Boxer Tricks*

In addition to the basic commands and a few helpful everyday words to teach your Boxer, you might also want to teach him a few tricks. They're fun to do and he will most likely enjoy them, too.

Here are a few favorite tricks that are very easy to work on; however, keep your eyes open for any other potential tricks your Boxer might excel at. For example, if he enjoys spinning around in circles, you can "teach" him to spin on command by giving the command *"Spin"* or *"Dizzy dog"* whenever you catch him spinning naturally. A reward and praise will cement the link between the verbal command and behavior over a period of time.

The following tricks do, for the most part, require your Boxer to be steady in a few of the basic commands, such as *"Sit"* and *"Down."* Make sure you have the preliminary commands mastered before adding the building blocks necessary to accomplish the trick.

Speak and Hush

Some dog owners worry that teaching their dogs to "speak" or bark on command will create a dog that won't stop barking. While this *could* happen, if you spend an equal amount of time teaching your Boxer to stop barking or *hush* on command, this shouldn't be too much of a problem.

Speak

The *speak* command can be quite an entertaining trick. If you teach a very subtle hand signal for the command (and your Boxer is *really* tuned in to hand signals), you can have him "answer" questions with a bark, or amazingly "count" with barks.

Boxers can be taught to do literally anything!

The *speak* command can serve a more serious role, too. If part of the reason that you purchased a Boxer was to deter strangers, teaching him to speak can create the appearance of a protective dog—without having any fear of accidental aggression. How does this work? When you teach your Boxer to speak, cue him with another, more serious command, such as *"Watch him!"* The threatening stranger will have no idea that your Boxer is barking away with a happy bark rather than a defensive bark; only *you* will be able to tell the difference.

Teaching the Speak

1. Start with a quiet Boxer that isn't barking.
2. Find a way to make him "play bark." For example, if he likes food, one of the easiest ways to get him to bark can be to playfully tease him with a favorite toy or a bit of food. (Your body language is important, too, in that you must relate to him that you're happy and ready to play but won't play until he barks.) For other Boxers, it may be as simple as just a certain "look" that gets him all wound up. Whatever works for you and your dog, as long as it's fun and positive (*never* anything that is frightening or painful!), try to get him to bark.
3. Time the command with the bark. When you see a bark coming—and if you're around your Boxer you pretty well know what that looks like—give the command *"Bark," "Speak,"* or *"Watch him!"*

4. Praise and treat your Boxer when he barks, even if he gives just a little "woof" and not a full bark. This will come!
5. Add a hand signal. As your Boxer learns to bark on command, add a hand signal, which can be as simple and subtle as touching your chin or raising your index finger up and down. When he learns the hand signal, fade away the voice command.
6. Follow up the bark command with a *hush* command (see the following).
7. Do not reward "free" barking. Boxers are really wily canines, and if a Boxer links together the fact that he can get a treat every time you tell him to bark, he may just try barking on his own to see if *that* pleases you, too—and that might mean a treat for him. Whatever you do, don't treat him for barking unless you've given him the command to bark.

If your Boxer is barking on his own for a treat, ignore him. Give him the *hush* command (if you've taught him this) or wait until he is quiet, then reward him.

Hush

Equally as important when teaching your pet the *speak* command, is training him to *stop* barking. He needs to learn that he can get treats and praise for being quiet when you ask him, too. Teaching the *hush* command requires a bit of timing and some patience, but it can be taught through positive reinforcement and repetition.

While your Boxer is barking, give him the *hush* hand signal and verbal command.

Training the Hush

1. Catch your Boxer when he's quiet. If you've given him the *speak* command and he has barked, you have also rewarded him for speaking. While he is holding his toy in his mouth or munching on his treat, say *"Hush"* and reward him again.
2. If you'd like, add a hand signal, such as the classic index finger to the lips, to the verbal command *"Hush."* Gradually fade the verbal command away while continuing to reinforce the hand signal with treats.
3. Do not reward barking when the *hush* command has been given. If necessary, put him in a *down-stay* and then give the command *"Hush."* It is very difficult for a dog to bark while in a *down,* and this may be the edge you need to get your Boxer to *hush.*

4. You can also use a treat to help silence your Boxer. Hold a treat in the palm of a closed hand and allow him to smell your hand while you give the command *"Hush."* It is *very* hard for him to bark while sniffing. At the moment he stops barking, reward him with the treat.

Play Dead (Roll Over) or Bang!

If you've got a Boxer that loves to clown around—and a dog that enjoys his treats—this can be a fairly easy trick to teach. As with other tricks, it takes some patience and timing, and of course, lots of praise!

Teaching the Roll-Over

1. Put your Boxer in a *down.*
2. With a treat in one hand, hold the treat under your Boxer's nose, then move it slowly back toward one shoulder, around toward the shoulder blades, to encourage him to roll over on his back. As he contorts a bit to follow the treat, or if he is a natural clown, he should be legs up and on his back.

Note: If you're working with a small puppy, you can actually help roll the pup over a little—if he's willing.

3. Say the command, *"Play dead"* or *"Bang!"* when your dog is on his back.
4. The hand signal should be, of course, a finger pointing like a gun!

Once you've taught your Boxer to flip on his back when you say *"Bang,"* you can add the hand signal to complete the trick.

5. As your dog masters this trick, he may even be able to drop from a standing position to the "dead dog" position for an even more dramatic show.

Note: If your Boxer is a bit fearful or perhaps a bit dominant, this trick may be difficult to teach initially. The reason for this is that dogs that do not trust their masters completely tend to be hesitant to expose their underbellies. (Lying on the back is a submissive gesture that is not seen often in dominant dogs, or in dogs too fearful to lie in such a vulnerable position.)

The *shake* is easy to teach to a dog that knows his *sit* command.

Shake

Some Boxers do this trick quite naturally. (A raised paw is considered a submissive gesture, so this exercise may also be a little more difficult at first with a more dominant dog.) Even if he doesn't readily give up his paw for a shake, you can teach him to do this quite easily.

Teaching the Shake

1. Put your Boxer in a *sit-stay.*
2. Grasp him by one of his forelegs and gently raise his leg up while saying *"Shake."*
3. Shake his paw a couple of times, and release his paw so that it drops back down to the floor, and praise!
4. Repetition makes perfect. Keep practicing!

After your dog knows you want his head between his paws when you say *"So sorry,"* he can be taught to do this in virtually any position.

So Sorry

We all know just how sorry a Boxer can look when he's done something that he knows he shouldn't have; the expression is priceless. This trick can't reproduce the genuine emotions of a "sorry" Boxer, but it can mimic some of the traits of a sorry dog.

Training the So Sorry

1. Sit on a chair with your Boxer at your side.

2. Encourage him to put his front paws on your leg.

3. Hold a treat between his front legs so that he has to dip his muzzle between his forelegs to get the treat, and say the command *"Sorry!"* or *"Say you're sorry!"*

4. When your Boxer readily associates *sorry* with this maneuver, transpose this trick to other areas, such as the edge of the bed, or a couch, or even the floor. He can even do this trick while standing with his front end down, head between the legs, and rear end up.

11 *Aggression*

Aggression among domestic dogs is a national problem. The Centers for Disease Control estimate that there are more than 4.7 million dog bite injuries each year. Most of these bites are not from loose or feral dogs, but rather these bite statistics are from family-owned pets. Children make up to 60 percent of dog bite victims and dog bite injuries continue to be the number one health concern for children under the age of 12. There has been at least one fatality attributed to a dog bite incident with a Boxer.

Before you panic, however, the Boxer is one of several breeds that is recognized for a wonderful, steady temperament and is *not* known to be an aggressive dog.

This bit of good news does not mean that the Boxer owner or breeder can be complacent about temperament and potential aggression problems. If the prediction is true that irresponsible dog owners will try to make the intimidating-looking but fun-loving Boxer the "bad dog" of the next decade, we could see some real changes in the Boxer temperament. As animal behaviorists note, it is possible to both breed in and breed out undesirable temperament characteristics. If irresponsible Boxer owners choose to breed dogs with poor temperaments, there will undoubtably be a rise in aggression problems within the breed.

Additionally, research has shown that a poor rearing environment can turn an otherwise friendly, outgoing puppy into a fearful, aggressive, or even snarling danger as an adult. So, the environment in which a Boxer is raised is almost equally as important as her genetic background when it comes to aggression. For these reasons, it is important that all Boxer owners and potential Boxer owners understand what aggression is, the many forms it can take, and the way to prevent or reduce these behaviors.

What Is Aggression?

In the wild, aggression is a natural response by wolves to a variety of situations. Though the wolf and the domestic dog are separated by thousands of years of selective breeding, aggression remains a natural response of the domestic dog in some situations. Because humans have had centuries to work on breeding out undesirable aggressiveness in domestic dogs, such as predatory behavior, a dog's aggressive responses are typically less intense and occur less frequently than with wolves. Domestication is an ongoing process, however, and as with trying to achieve the perfectly conformed Boxer, perfection is a bit illusive.

So, while we'd like to think our Boxers are all perfect and wonderful, this is not true. As mentioned earlier, the majority of Boxers today are very well tempered; however, with the Boxer's current enormous popularity, the sheer numbers alone with which this dog is being bred dictate a higher probability that some inappropriate, aggressive traits will be reintroduced or inadvertently emphasized. Compounding the numbers problem is the fact that wherever there is money to be made or trophies to be won, there will always be those who will throw temperament concerns to the wind in exchange for an opportunity to make some money (puppies, puppies, and more puppies!), or a misdirected quest for the picture-perfect Boxer with no concern for temperament.

Animal behaviorists seem to agree that the basis for aggression is in the dog's genetics, and therefore, breeders have an incredible responsibility to make sure that the Boxer maintains its reputation as one of the most gentle and nonaggressive dogs bred today. To shirk this responsibility and to breed bad-tempered or just quirky Boxers is a huge disservice to the breed.

Perhaps the German Boxer Club really struck upon something decades ago by requiring a good temperament as part of their breeding suitability requirements. Since the American Kennel Club (AKC) and the American Boxer Club (ABC) have no similar requirement in the United States, it becomes a personal responsibility of the breeder to breed equally for

The fact that the Boxer is so popular, and yet has so few bite incidents reported, is a real testament to this breed's steady temperament.

temperament, conformation, and performance. The result is that there are excellent, conscientious Boxer breeders in the United States who are doing everything right, but it is up to the potential Boxer owner to find these breeders when trying to purchase a quality puppy.

Nature vs. Nurture

Many forms of aggression are believed to have a genetic base. With the knowledge that a dog is predisposed to certain forms of aggression, the cards are *still* stacked in the owner's favor. As noted earlier in this book, it is estimated that as much as 40 percent or more of the dog's final temperament is a direct result of her environment. This is a significant amount of influence! If the owner is aware of what is and what isn't aggressive behavior, and can recognize any aggressive tendencies *early* in the Boxer puppy's life, he or she should have good success in curbing these tendencies and successfully shaping a good-tempered Boxer.

Additionally, with a thorough understanding of aggression, Boxer owners can avoid inadvertently creating an aggression problem with their dogs. For example, the classic mistake made by many dog owners is to tie or chain their dogs to a stationary object in their backyard rather than spend the money to securely fence it. When on a chain, even the friendliest dog will have no place to hide and will eventually become defensive of her territory—if only in an act of self-preservation. (Chaining a dog to the front door was a documented method used and recommended by

Romans in the city of Pompeii to create guard dogs!) With no fence to keep critters and children out, and a dog that has become fearful or defensive of her property, the owner has created a dangerous dog. In fact, so potentially dangerous that one study recorded that up to one third of all dog bite fatalities among children involved—you guessed it—*a dog on a chain in an unfenced backyard*.

Types of Aggressive Behavior

Now that you understand the influence that genetics and the environment can have on the development of aggression in a dog, it is important to recognize the different types of aggression, and what kinds of environmental factors are believed to affect these types of aggression.

Fear

Biting out of fear is thought to be the most common reason for dog bite injuries. When a dog is fearful, she is truly afraid for her life. When she is given no escape from her fear, the only defense (in her mind) is to show aggression in hopes of coming out alive. This could be a growl, snarl, snap, or even a full-fledged bite.

Fear aggression is thought to be largely hereditary, and dogs can inherit their fearfulness from either or both parents. A Boxer that is not predisposed to fearfulness can become fearful if exposed to very frightening events as a puppy, or from not being socialized properly. For

Not only is this Boxer not fearful, he also allows anyone to come up and pet him while he is lying by his "prize" during a Schutzhund training session.

If raised in a good environment and properly socialized with all different types of dogs, dog-dog aggression is generally not a problem for the Boxer.

example, a puppy may develop a fear of men if she is abused by a man as a puppy. If the puppy is kept in isolation from people, she can develop a fear of people in general. Or, if the puppy has limited exposure to people, she may develop a fear of certain types of people, such as men with baseball hats, young children or toddlers, elderly people with walkers, or people of races different from the owner's.

Dog-Dog

If you are walking your Boxer and the mere presence of *any* strange dog produces a lunging, growling, "hackles up" response from your Boxer, this is dog-dog aggression. In Boxers, as in most other breeds, this form of aggression occurs most frequently in unneutered males, but can and does occur in females, too.

Generally, dog-dog aggression is thought to be genetically based; however, animal behaviorists note that there are many environmental factors that can strongly influence how tolerable or intolerable this behavior becomes. Some forms of dog-dog aggression can occur in nonaggressive Boxers if the dog, for example, was attacked by another dog as a puppy.

Fortunately, dogs that are inherently aggressive as well as those that have developed an aggression as a result of an incident generally are not considered hopeless. Behaviorists say that dog-dog aggression has one of the best "rehabilitation" success rates if the owner begins working with the puppy immediately (see What Does Work, page 97).

Territorial

Some breeds are more territorial than others, particularly those that were bred specifically to guard people, livestock, or property. The Boxer is recognized as a great watchdog but not a particularly stellar guard dog ("Got a cookie? Cool. Let me show you where they keep the jewels . . . "). For this reason, the Boxer generally doesn't have problems with territorial aggression; however, this may not be true for *your* Boxer. As with dog-dog aggression, territorial aggression, though largely inherited, can be compounded by environmental factors.

Chaining a dog in the yard, as discussed earlier, is a classic example of creating a dog that feels she must defend herself or her property. An owner's reactions to a dog's territorial behaviors can also escalate territorial aggression. If a

If a dog is allowed to run a fence line and bark at anybody or anything on the other side, she may think she is successfully chasing the "foe" away and become even more territorial.

dog growls and barks at strangers entering the home, and the owner pats the dog in an attempt to calm her down or speaks to her in reassuring tones ("It's O.K., sweetie"), the owner is reinforcing this territorial behavior.

Other environmental factors that can reinforce territoriality in a dog is to allow her to "chase off" intruders from the property. If she is allowed to run the fence line barking at passing dogs, in her mind she has chased off the dogs because they have "left" her property. The same goes for chasing cars or children on bicycles.

Territorial aggression is currently the most common problem for which dog owners seek help at animal behavior clinics. Animal behaviorists note that they don't feel this is because territorial problems never existed before, but because dog owners are more aware of (and more susceptible to) potential law suits and vicious dog laws than they were years ago.

Resource or Possession Guarding

This is not a common form of aggression among Boxers, but for the safety of the owner, and the owner's family and friends, it is a form of aggression that should not be tolerated and should be prevented or modified to make the situation safe for anyone who enters the home. So, what is resource or possession guarding? It is the growling, snarling, snapping, or biting of a dog when any of her possessions are taken away, or if she perceives (accurately

or inaccurately) that someone *wants* to take her possessions away.

Resource or possession guarding may flair up only when the Boxer is given a particularly scrumptious bone, a favorite toy, or perhaps her food. Though resource or possession guarding is a natural behavior among and between dogs, it cannot be tolerated when this aggression is directed at people. Some behaviorists feel that resource or possession guarding is actually a subset of dominance aggression (see following information). In other words, acts of resource or possession guarding (i.e., biting a small child who attempts to pet the dog while she is eating) only occur if the dog sees that person as subordinate.

Dominance

To bite or threaten the very person the Boxer adores is an act that the vast majority of Boxers would never even consider. However, there are a few dogs that are born leaders that don't take well to the fact that they must be subordinate to *someone*. Given any opportunity to rule the house, these dogs will take the lead and run with it. Even when they accept a human as the leader, they may continually test and control less assertive family members, typically children.

Then there are other dogs that aren't naturally dominant, but when raised in an unstructured environment and not given any clear-cut leadership (i.e., they are thrust into the leadership role), the dogs will attempt to become the dominant figure in the household.

> **Boxer Byte:** If your adult Boxer has been a sweetie all her life and suddenly begins behaving aggressively, make sure that before you jump to conclusions, your veterinarian has ruled out any physical pain or illnesses. Ear infections, dental problems, deafness (if the dog is badly startled), hip dysplasia, arthritis, and blindness are all conditions that could induce your Boxer to respond abnormally.

In either case, if the situation is allowed to progress to the point at which warning growls or snarls have turned into full-fledged bites, the owner has a serious problem. Dominance-aggression bites are typically on the face of the human or the top of the head, the same locations a dog would naturally use to give a warning squeeze to a subordinate dog. The only problem is that a human's head, particularly that of a small or young child, is not bony like a dog's. The dog continues to apply pressure until she feels "bone," which can have tragic and/or fatal consequences with a human.

Compounding this problem is that the way a person typically reacts to canine aggression is the reverse of a dog's natural reaction: The human screams in panic and flails around trying to escape; the dog's reaction is to be motionless and quiet or perhaps whimper or yip. The human's response only further confuses the dog, who sees the actions as a confrontation.

Successful rehabilitation of a dog that has been allowed to become dominant-aggressive is very slim, according to researchers. The only real chance an owner has of turning this dog into a safe, controllable pet is to catch the early warning signs of dominance aggression and prevent them from escalating. Warning signs include:

- A puppy/dog that growls or snaps when given a command
- A puppy/dog that dislikes being touched, leaned on, stepped over, moved, or generally disturbed
- Resource or possession guarding

Though the Boxer who is raised with children usually smothers them in kisses, the dog must realize that she can't dominate even little children.

- Protection of a particular family member or dog "friend" from other family members
- Positioning herself and threatening the owner so that he or she can't leave the room

Predatory Behavior

Since this behavior is stimulated by a totally different set of hormones than the forms of aggression listed earlier, some behaviorists argue that predation is not a form of aggression at all. Rather, they say it is a "behavior." Regardless of what

95

Boxer Byte: If you have a behavior problem involving aggression, you should seek qualified help. There are two ways to find this help.

Veterinary animal behaviorists. A veterinary behaviorist is a veterinarian who works with both behavior modification and prescription medications, and is certified by the American College of Veterinary Behaviorists. Unfortunately, there are very few veterinary behaviorists in the United States, and finding one in your area may be very difficult unless you live near a veterinary school. To locate a veterinary animal behaviorist, ask your veterinarian for a recommendation, or contact the American Veterinary Medical Association for a referral at: AVMA, 1931 North Meacham Road (Suite 100), Schaumburg, IL 60173, Phone: 847-925-8070, Fax: 847-925-1329; E-mail: AVMAINFO@avma.org; (*www.avma.org*)

Certified animal behaviorist. A certified animal behaviorist holds a doctoral degree (Ph.D.) in animal behavior and is certified by the Animal Behavior Society as capable of working with animal behavior problems. To find an animal behaviorist in your area, or to check an animal behaviorist's credentials, contact the Animal Behavior Society at: American Editorial Office for Animal Behavior, 2611 East 10th Street, #170, Indiana University, Bloomington, IN 47408-2603; Phone: (812) 856-5541; Fax: (812) 856-5542; web site: *http://www.animalbehavior.org/ABS/*

category it fits into, predatory behavior toward humans is entirely unacceptable. Fortunately, it is a behavior that humans have tried to breed out of domestic dogs, and as a result, it is extremely rare.

Animal behaviorists warn, however, that if an owner sees that his or her dog tends to kill cats—and not just give them a good chase—the owner should be *particularly* cautious with this dog around human infants. The jerking movements of a baby, coupled with high-pitched screams, could trigger a predatory reaction from the dog. Stalking or growling at a baby should be considered extreme warning signs.

What Doesn't Work

In animal behavior and dog training, as in many other fields, popular opinion about the correct way to handle things can change dramatically from decade to decade. Handling aggressive behavior is a good example. Though behaviorists vary widely in their interpretations of aggression (some classify aggression in as many as ten categories) and the causes of aggression (the nature vs. nurture question), most animal behaviorists seem united in declaring that violent, physical methods of handling aggression are useless and only worsen the problem.

For a while, some behaviorists and quite a few books espoused the theory that domestic dogs could not adequately interpret human language—both verbal and body—and therefore, the owner must "speak" dog and "act" dog. Of course, as discussed in an earlier chapter, we now know better and acknowledge that our dogs (particularly Boxers) are very adept at reading our body language and can and do understand key words in our language.

But, in the darker ages, many trainers were promoting the "scruff shake" and "dominance roll" techniques to handle aggression. Though these strategies are becoming less frequently seen, it is important for the Boxer owner to understand why they shouldn't ever be used, in case a trainer or friend recommends them.

The scruff shake. The scruff shake, for those who are lucky enough not to have been exposed to this, is when the owner physically grabs the dog's scruff, gets up in the dog's face, and makes fierce growling noises. This method, purportedly modeled after wolf behavior, was supposed to establish dominance. What it did, in actuality, was get a lot of owners bitten. The fearful dog felt threatened and probably bit in what she thought was self-defense; the truly dominant dog reacted to the direct threat by fighting.

The dominance roll. The dominance roll, in which the owner was told to roll an aggressive dog over into a submissive position (on the back, belly exposed), was another training folly. Again, if the dog's

aggression was fear-based, this action would frighten her even more and often caused an increased struggle or bite. With a truly dominant dog, the dominance roll would serve only to escalate the problem.

As animal behaviorists who have spent their lives studying wolves relate, wolves themselves rarely resort to these forms of physical, violent acts of dominance. Theirs is much more ritualized, with little true aggression shown between pack members. Beyond this, domestic dogs have been bred to resemble their wolf progenitors in very few ways. Physical dominance, to put it plainly, just doesn't work.

What Does Work: Handling Aggression

So what does work? If your Boxer is growling and lunging at strange dogs on walks, or if your puppy snarls when you attempt to retrieve your shoe from her crate, what do you do? Your best approach is to know what to do before the aggressive situation ever presents itself. By knowing exactly how to respond to a situation, any inappropriate behaviors will not be reinforced. Secondly, you should seek professional help. Aggression in *any* form is a serious issue. And behaviorists say that dogs with an aggression problem rarely have just one form; it's kind of a mixed bag. So, the owner will need to take great care to make sure the puppy or dog receives proper training and handling to keep any aggressive tendencies at bay.

The following are some common aggression problems and techniques commonly recommended to prevent and reduce them. These techniques are best performed under the supervision of a trained and certified animal behaviorist, and the explanation of these techniques in no way is intended to take the place of counseling with an animal behaviorist.

A dog in a firm *down-stay* is less likely to bark or growl at another dog or person, and is also less likely to lunge. The *down* is a submissive position and helps to affirm the leadership of the owner.

Fear-based Aggression

Fear-based aggression, for the most part, can be avoided in Boxers that are not predisposed genetically to be fearful. As long as the Boxer is well socialized with all kinds of people, dogs, and situations, she should develop into a happy and outgoing Boxer. If a puppy has inherited a fearful temperament, the owner will have more challenges to raise this dog into a normal Boxer; however, if her experiences are kept positive and she is socialized at an early age, she *can* develop into a sociable Boxer.

The best way to produce an outgoing or less fearful Boxer is to set up her experiences so that they are positive by socializing her with a variety of people and dogs (see The Shy Boxer, page 40).

Note: Owners of very fearful dogs, or those that tend to get their "hackles up" over any new person or situation, should seek professional help for them and the Boxer. An owner should never put an innocent person in danger while trying to socialize the dog.

Dog-Dog Aggression

With puppies, it is important to make sure the Boxer is introduced to other puppies and only gentle, *safe* adult dogs, the type of dogs that would never show aggression to the puppy (see Socializing Your Puppy with Other Dogs, page 43). Socializing the Boxer puppy with other puppies and dogs in a controlled setting ensures that she is comfortable playing with many other types of dogs. It also prevents dog-dog aggression that is fear-based from developing.

If a Boxer is not introduced to other puppies and gentle dogs while she is developing, she can become uncertain or frightened by them. If she has a bad experience, such as being bitten or ferociously chased by an adult dog, this experience can also lead to fear-based, dog-dog aggression. So, screening your Boxer's canine friends is quite important!

Neutering and Desensitization

In other cases, particularly with intact males, the aggression shown toward other dogs is *not* fear-based. In these cases, neutering is successful in eliminating or greatly reducing aggression.

In combination with neutering, behaviorists also commonly recommend a *desensitization* program to teach a dog not to be so aggressive. These programs frequently require the handler to put the Boxer in a *sit-stay* on a loose leash, so the dog doesn't become aggressive just because she senses your nervousness, and when the approaching dog nears, the owner is to talk happily with the Boxer, as in, "Oh, look! Another dog is coming this way. Doesn't he look like fun?" Reward her with a food treat for sitting quietly (or giving a rump wiggle). Do not reward barking or lunging and breaking the *sit-stay*, and at this point, turn around and walk the dog away.

In very difficult cases, a behaviorist may recommend that the dog wears a muzzle when in public, and/or may prescribe medications. If this is the case, you should balance the liability of the dog, and the safety of the neighborhood animals with your ability to keep the dog safely.

Territorial Behavior

As previously discussed, a dog of any breed can become territorial. Unfortunately, territorial tendencies can be inadvertently reinforced and compounded by the owner. A dog that barks at passing people should not be allowed outside

Boxer Byte: Dog-dog aggressive Boxers should not be allowed to investigate strange dogs. They should be taught to *ignore* other dogs, and pay attention to you. If you want to introduce your Boxer on leash to a new dog, and you know she tends to be dog-dog aggressive, take the precaution of using a muzzle or head halter and watch her body language very carefully. Also, be absolutely sure that you can handle her strength if she decides to disregard your commands and lunge. If while meeting a new dog, her body begins to stiffen, put her into a *down*. The *down* is a submissive position and also one in which the dog has difficulties barking or growling.

Also, be sure to watch your body language. If you're worried your dog might act aggressively, she will pick up on your concerns and may direct your fear into aggression toward what she thinks you fear—the approaching dog. Her aggression in this case may be directly due to your fears!

> **Boxer Byte:** If your Boxer is barking and lunging, never pull back so sharply on her leash that you raise her front legs off the ground. A dog with her front paws in the air will be interpreted as aggressive posturing by the other dog and will cause this dog to feel even more threatened.

unless you are present to supervise. If the territorial aggression is displayed when people come to the door, behaviorists commonly recommend that the dog be trained to obey a *down-stay* at the door when a person is approaching. The dog is then rewarded with food treats for remaining in the *down-stay.* If the dog attempts to bark or lunge (she will have to break the *down-stay* to do this), she should be put back into the *down-stay,*

Resource guarding: Most Boxers will give up their treasured toys and "stolen" finds when asked (or when finally caught); but if your Boxer growls or snaps to avoid giving up an item, you'll need to work with her.

and this obedience should be rewarded with verbal praise.

This exercise can be "set up" with a willing neighbor or an understanding dog owner. The more it is repeated, the more the appropriate behaviors will be reinforced.

Resource or Possession Guarding

The best way to limit this behavior is to prevent it from ever beginning or to catch the problem early while the Boxer is still a puppy. Preventive exercises include eating before you feed your puppy (reinforcing that the puppy is lower in status than family members), making her sit before you put her food bowl down, and petting her while she is eating (and *not* growling), tossing little tidbits into the bowl while she is eating from time to time, and occasionally picking up the bowl, putting the puppy back in a *sit,* and then putting the bowl back down. Favorite toys and chews should also be "exchanged" for a yummy treat, then handed back.

If the Boxer already has a resource or possession guarding problem—and remember, this is considered to be a dominance-related behavior—care should be taken to prevent confrontations. If she is protective of only one particular chew, don't let her have this chew, and practice swapping other chews with treats. If she growls when someone approaches her food, begin hand-feeding her and making her "work" for her food through *sits* and *downs.* If you do feed a portion in the bowl, make sure that she is safely away from children and in her crate.

Dominance Behavior

Though dominance aggression problems are one of the most common behavioral problems cited by owners seeking help, fortunately it is a problem that is not seen with any great frequency in Boxers. With this in mind, however, it is advisable for *all* Boxer owners to be assertive leaders to their dogs and to have the mind-set necessary to prevent dominance problems from occurring. In breeds that have problems with dominance, breeders and rescue agencies concur that generally 15 to 20 minutes of obedience work a day—beginning as a tiny puppy and continuing *through the dog's entire life*—keeps the predisposed, dominant dog from attempting to usurp the owner's leadership.

If you allow the dominance factor to escalate into aggression toward you, the situation is serious and should be handled only under the close supervision of a veterinary animal behaviorist or a certified animal behaviorist (see Where to Get Help, page 96). If you are willing to work with the behaviorist in reshaping the dog's behaviors and perhaps administering prescription, behavior modifying drugs, the dog *may* make progress.

Predatory Behavior

This behavior is so rare in dogs in general—and even rarer in our gentle Boxers—that it hardly merits mentioning here. There is nothing that can be done to modify this behavior if it appears. Owners of a dog that is seen growling or stalking a baby or young child should make sure the dog is *never* allowed contact with this age

group, and, unfortunately, euthanasia may be the owner's best and safest option after a complete evaluation from a qualified behavioral specialist.

Prevention Is the Best Bet

Aggression is scary stuff, but prevention and early intervention are the best approaches. Providing a positive environment, knowing and understanding the early signs of aggression, and seeking experienced professional help are all factors that can help when dealing with aggressive behaviors.

If, after doing everything right and seeking professional help, your Boxer cannot be trusted not to bite, you must make a difficult decision. If you can guarantee that she will *never* have the opportunity to bite someone, and you can securely contain her to ensure this, then perhaps you can avoid euthanasia. If, however, you cannot ensure that she will never be in a position to bite someone, the best decision for you and your dog might be to humanely allow it to cross the bridge, albeit a bit early.

There are so many Boxers in this world that possess the essential essence of Boxers—the happy, rump-wiggling, kidney bean-dancing dogs that have made this breed so popular—that the line must be drawn as to when we finally give up on one that is truly dangerous.

If you do your research, screen for good Boxer parents, and then raise your puppy in a positive environment from *the beginning*, you should have the wonderful Boxer experience you deserve!

101

12 *Looking for Trouble*

When you combine the Boxer's extreme intelligence, high activity level, and uncanny sense of humor, you have a dog that must be kept active both physically and mentally. If he isn't, he will find ways to keep himself amused. Unfortunately, the types of things a Boxer tends to think up to keep himself busy rarely amuses his owner. In other words, a bored Boxer, as you might already know, can be a destructive thing.

Idle Boxers have been known to chew, bark, dig, climb, and jump. Because these dogs are so athletic and strong, they tend to perform these destructive activities with great skill, too. That means that the entire couch instead of just a pillow, is shredded, the barking is louder, the holes are bigger and deeper, and fences are scaled with ease.

What's a poor Boxer owner to do?

The best way to solve any or all of these problems is to look beyond the symptoms (barking, digging, climbing, jumping) and treat the cause of the behavior. In other words, if you can figure out the reason *why* your Boxer is doing what he's doing, you most likely can cure or at least minimize the problem behavior.

Attention— the #1 Cure

The primary reason for inappropriate or unwanted behaviors in dogs is lack of attention. Initially, this seems like an easy fix—just spend more time with your Boxer. This is true, but only to a point. With so many dog owners working during

If not given enough attention or exercise, the Boxer will look for ways to amuse himself. Pictured here is "Spencer," who found some excellent dirt to dig in.

the day, there are an increasing number of dogs that have to be left alone during working hours. While they are alone, many of these dogs attempt to amuse themselves. To avoid destructive behavior, working owners can and do come up with a variety of creative methods to help their dogs.

1. **Give Your Dog a Break.** If you work close to your home, take your lunch hour with your Boxer. Go home, throw a ball, or take him for a walk. This will help to burn off a little of that Boxer energy and it's a great midday stress buster for you.

2. **Hire a Pet Walker.** Professional pet walkers are great; they take your dog to a local park, play ball with him, or just go for long walks. For an hour every day, he can frolic to his heart's content. This option doesn't come without a price, however. Pet walkers can charge up to $15 a visit for their services in larger cities. If you have a neighbor (perhaps someone is retired in your neighborhood?) or nearby relative who would enjoy walking your dog every day, you might be able to negotiate a better price.

3. **Consider a Doggie Day Care Facility.** This is a full-day service and requires a very sociable dog with no dog-dog aggression and good "pack" behaviors. Screen your day care facility carefully; not all are created equally. Charges are high for this service; you can expect to pay up to $20 a day or more in some areas.

4. **Load Up on Toys.** There are lots of durable, tough toys on the market that will keep your Boxer occupied for sometimes several hours at a time and that can be left safely in his crate when he's unsupervised. Particularly popular are large, hard rubber toys with slots that can be stuffed with biscuits or treats; he will work a long time to get those treats out!

5. **Buy a Crate.** If your Boxer has a serious tendency toward chewing, barking, digging, or climbing fences, crate him when you cannot supervise him. Most dogs enjoy their crates if they are given a comfortable surface to lie on and a good chew (see Crate Training, page 26).

6. **Leash Him.** If your Boxer looks for trouble *while* you are home, tie his leash to your belt so that you can have your hands and mind free to attend to other things, but also have a physical tie to him. In other words, he can't run and rip up a couch cushion if he's by your side.

Indoor and Outdoor Behavior Problems

Sometimes you can be doing the best job anyone could hope to do as an owner, and your Boxer will still find ways to wreak havoc in your home and yard. The following are some tips and training tools for several of the most commonly cited Boxer problems. These, of course, are guidelines—if your Boxer has a problem that extends beyond the scope of this chapter, it is best to ask the advice of a professional (see Where to Get Help, page 96).

Barking

Boxers don't tend to be barkers, but they can be vocal dogs. They are known for barking a resounding alert when someone has come to the front door. They also can bark for attention, or bark to guard their territory, or bark just for the sheer joy of barking.

- A good way to teach your Boxer when to stop barking in the home is by teaching the dog the *speak* and *hush* commands (see Speak and Hush, page 84). If your dog knows he will be rewarded for sounding the alarm, as well as for quickly calming down and becoming silent, he will be much easier to quiet down when you want him to.
- If a dog is barking for attention, you need to take a look at your situation. Be honest. Are you giving this dog enough attention? Or, are you shortchanging him a little? If you are, try to increase your activity time with

Finding out *why* your Boxer is barking is the key to solving the problem.

him. Play ball in the backyard, allow him to follow you around the house and "help" with chores, take him on car rides, let the kids take him for walks (if they are ten or older and if he is good at walking on a leash).
- Remember, don't reinforce barking behavior. If he barks for attention, ignore him until he's quiet again, and then lavish the attention.

Exception. There's an exception to the "ignoring" method toward barking. If you attempt to keep him as an outside dog, he *will* bark and he will likely not stop barking until you let him inside the home. And, in this instance, he is right! The Boxer's place is by his owner's side and as a house pet, not a yard ornament. The reason for the barking in this instance is that he is not getting the care and attention he deserves and is letting his owner know.

Here are some tips on how to cure excessive barking.

- For the Boxer that can't resist barking at everything that goes by when he's outside in the yard, consider moving him away from what makes him bark. This may mean keeping him indoors during the day if you work, or indoors at night so as not to annoy the neighbors. (He should already be indoors at night!)
- Another option is to improve your dog's view of the world. If you have a privacy fence, your Boxer can *smell* and *hear* that something's out there, he just can't see what it is. Cutting a small knothole at his eye level every 6 feet

(1.8 m) or so along a solid fence will give him a chance to *see* what he senses. A chain link fence might be an option, too.

■ If all else fails, there are a variety of anti-bark collars on the market, including those that use citronella spray, high-pitched tones, and low electronic settings.

Chewing

Boxers are big on chewing. They chew as puppies during their teething phase. They chew as young adolescents just because it feels good and is fun. They chew as adults for the same reasons as adolescents, only now that they're fully grown, their bite, which is substantial, is capable of doing a lot of damage.

Chewing is a natural dog thing; it really isn't a bad habit at all—it keeps the dog's teeth clean and white—unless, of course, the Boxer is chewing on something inappropriate, such as your baseboards, leather shoes, or furniture. The good news is that chewing does not have to be a problem. There are several things you can do to help appease your Boxer's healthy appetite for chewing while rescuing your furniture and rugs.

■ Keep your Boxer satisfied with a variety of hard rubber chew toys, stuffable chew toys, knotted rope tugs, and hollow shinbones.

■ Rotate the toys and chews. If you can afford it, keep a bucket of about 12 different chews and toys but only let your dog play with 8 at a time. Pick the chews and toys up at night and

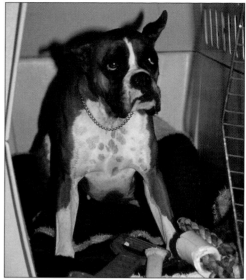

Λ good supply of chew toys will go far to satisfy your Boxer's natural chewing urges. A crate can help, too, when you absolutely can't watch what your Boxer is doing.

give your dog a different mix the next day.

■ Never leave your Boxer unattended. If you *know* you have an active chewer, be sure to crate him or confine him to a trouble-free area of the house when you can't keep your eye on him. Remember, this is a very curious and active dog. Just because something doesn't look like a chew toy to *you* (i.e., the arm of your favorite recliner or a seat belt in your car), doesn't mean it doesn't look like fun to your Boxer.

■ Keep any room your Boxer has access to picked up and free of loose items, such as shoes, socks, toys, books, newspapers, or magazines on the floor. Make sure the closet door is closed.

Flowers and plants aren't really ever safe from a Boxer unless you can keep the two separated.

- If your Boxer is honing in on one particular area of the house (perhaps chewing a certain corner of your kitchen cabinets), you can try applying a "no chew" type ointment or spray on the area. The ointment is harmless to dogs, but it has a bitter enough taste that dogs are generally repelled by it. If you are unfortunate enough to own a Boxer with "bad" taste or one with no taste at all, he may like or ignore the ointment, in which case you're back to square one—supervise or crate or contain him in a safe place.
- Don't "chew" on your Boxer for chewing something up. This won't keep him from chewing again! Remember, chewing is a natural urge. Your job is to channel this urge by giving him chewing-appropriate items and to supervise!

Digging

Boxers will generally dig for one of several reasons: to bury things, to dig things up (newly planted annuals nearly always need uprooting), to escape underneath a fence, to find a cool spot in the yard on a hot day, or just for the fun of it. Bored dogs may dig more, but it's probably safer to say that unsupervised Boxers dig the most.

If you have a digging dog, there are several things you can try to put a damper on the digging.

- Bring your dog inside. If he's not outside, he can't dig.
- Supervise your dog. When your Boxer *is* outside, watch him. If he starts to dig, tell him *"No!"* or *"Ah-Ah!"* Then distract him with a constructive game of catch or a controlled game of tug.
- Barricade your yard. If you don't want your Boxer relandscaping for you, build a side yard just for your dog, or protect your plants with an additional fence. Sometimes invisible fences—electric fences buried under the ground that work with a collar—within a large backyard can be very effective in keeping your Boxer in just the areas you want him.
- Make a digging pit. Now this is only for the brave owner, but it does work for dogs that dig solely to bury and unearth treasures. Construct a 4 × 4 foot (122 × 122 cm) area of soft dirt or sand and bury bones for him. Praise him when he digs and buries things in this area, and prevent him from doing this elsewhere in the yard. (This requires supervision.)

■ Take the fun out of digging. If your dog is digging to escape under a fence, make sure the areas at the base of the fence are not fun or easy to dig. Large, heavy, rough rocks could make a good border to prevent diggers from escaping.

Climbing

This habit is a frustrating one. It is safe to say that Boxers often scale enormous and seemingly impossible fences just to get to the other side. Unneutered male Boxers are probably the worst offenders and will go to great lengths to leave any form of enclosure if they sense there's a female in season even remotely close to them. Fence climbing is a dangerous sport for a Boxer, and a loose Boxer is very likely to be hit by a car.

If you have a fence climbing Boxer, take heart; there are some ways to dampen your dog's abilities.

■ Alter your Boxer. If you have a male, neuter him. If you have a female, spay her. With no hormonal drive, your Boxer's wanderlust will be dampened.
■ Heighten your fencing. If your fence is only 4-feet (122-cm) tall, this is a piece of cake for your Boxer. Raise it to 6 feet (183 cm) and see if you can stop the problem.
■ Change your fencing. If you have chain link, your Boxer may be able to get a foothold in the links. Consider changing your fencing to a board fence so he can't get a toehold to begin scaling.

■ Add a slant. If you already have a board fence that your Boxer is climbing, consider reinstalling it with a slight slant *into* the yard. This makes it impossible for him to climb.
■ Charge it. Add an invisible fence and collar system to your already existing fence, but remember, if you have a lot of storms that knock out your power, when the power's down, so is your fence. Also, some Boxers may be so determined to scale the fence, they might suffer the charge just to get out.
■ Put a lip or lid on it. You can try adding a 2-foot (61-cm) "lip" of chain link (if you have a metal fence) or wood to the top of your fence to keep your Boxer contained. Or, if you have a chain link fence, you could consider creating a shaded run area or side yard with a chain link cover to keep your errant

The Boxer's athleticism can be frustrating, but a higher fence and neutering may help to dampen this male Boxer's wanderlust.

107

Boxer contained when you can't supervise his outdoor play time.

■ Lock him up. Boxers are notoriously good escape artists and this includes an uncanny ability to open gates, twist doorknobs, or do whatever it takes to free themselves. Make sure your gates latches are locked securely.

Note: A tie-out should never be used with a Boxer for several reasons. First, the Boxer is so strong that if he hits the end of the cable at full strength, he can pull up the stake, and/or severely injure himself. Additionally, an unsupervised dog on a tie-out is inviting trouble. If your Boxer doesn't successfully strangle himself (if the cable is attached to his collar), or injure a leg by wrapping the cable around himself, he might very well develop aggressive tendencies (see Territorial Aggression, page 93).

People Problems

For the Boxer, any unwanted behavior problems that affect people generally stem from his unbridled enthusiasm or his profound love and affection for people. These behaviors are typical for a dog, but they must be reined in to make him a pet that can be enjoyed by all people.

Jumping Up

The airborne, full-tongue slurp is classic Boxer. This is what Boxer owners live for. There can't possibly be a breed with a warmer, more enthusiastic, know-no-limits

kind of welcome. However, if you are dressed and ready for work, carrying in a load of groceries, or introducing a frailer family member to your Boxer, then jumping up becomes a problem.

So, recognizing that the Boxer bounce is a sign of affection, you will want to teach him restraint without dampening his spirits. Here are some tips on how to accomplish this.

■ Teach your Boxer the *kisses/hugs* command (see page 82). This will allow you to control him when you need to, and allow him to express his affections at a more appropriate time.

■ Reinforce the *sit* command (see page 65). If you don't want to allow your Boxer to jump *ever,* make sure you can give him an activity for which he can be rewarded and praised. If he is steady on his *sits,* tell him to sit whenever he is getting the wild urge to jump or whenever he is greeting people. When he sits, reward him calmly, or have the person he is greeting reward him with a treat. Your Boxer will quickly learn that he gets the attention he wants if he sits. You will find that your Boxer, when coming up on a group of people, may actually sit just so he can get the anticipated attention.

■ Leash him. If your Boxer tends to jump up on your children, one way to have quick control over him is to allow him to drag a light leash in the house. Of course, this must be done *only* when you are home and supervising him; otherwise, he will injure or strangle himself. When he runs up to your child, step on the leash to stop him from jumping, then put him in a *sit* or a *down.* Reward him when he obeys. He will soon learn that he only gets pats and rewards when he sits or lies down for your children.

Nipping and Mouthing

If there is one puppy complaint that seems to exist for all breeds, it is that the puppy is nipping or chewing on his owners. Boxers are no exception to this complaint. Boxers are, as already noted, a breed that likes to chew a lot, and puppies need to learn that human hands, feet, legs, clothing, and shoes are *not* on the list of nippable items. Those little white teeth are like needles and they hurt! And, you don't want this behavior to continue as an adult dog.

There are several gentle ways to teach your puppy not to chew on you. The following provide some tips to help you get started working with your puppy to curb his nipping tendencies and to continue to teach him what is called "bite inhibition."

- Be a dog. No, you don't have to go down on all fours, but when your puppy nips you, let him know it hurts you—yelp. That's right. Let loose a loud *"Ow!"* or *"Ay!"* and then *ignore* your puppy. If you don't play with him, this defeats the purpose of his play bite.
- Provide an alternate behavior. If your puppy or adult is bouncing up and nipping you, tell him *"Ow!"* followed by a *sit* command. Reward a good *sit* with calm praise and then release him, *calmly.*

Teaching a steady *sit-stay* will prevent your Boxer from jumping up on people when they enter the front door.

- Bite this! If you know your Boxer will greet you with nips, head him off at the pass and provide an alternative chew that is constructive. Have a bone or chew toy ready and, giving him the *take it* command (see Take It, page 79), hand the toy to him *before* he starts nipping you. Often this is enough to head off the nips. After providing a toy several times, you may find that he will actually fetch a toy and bring it to you when he sees you.
- Burn it off. A lot of horsing around can be minimized by allowing your Boxer lots of opportunity to burn off his extra

energy. A tired Boxer is often a content Boxer!

■ Use time-outs judiciously. If the nipping and mouthing are part of your Boxer's wild greetings, you may want to use his crate (without toys) for a few minutes as a calming area. Do not drag him to the crate as a punishment. Simply coax him gently and calmly to his area and allow him to settle down in the crate.

Note: Puppy nips and even gentle mouthing by adults are not generally considered aggressive behavior; however, be aware that nipping and mouthing may escalate to play biting or even more serious dominant behaviors. If your Boxer shows any signs of being aggressive (see Aggression, pages 89–101), seek professional help immediately. Many forms of aggression can be effectively nipped in the bud if appropriate action is taken immediately.

Separation Anxiety

Can a Boxer love his owner too much? Parting with your Boxer for even a few minutes is not such "sweet sorrow" if it means that your canine transforms into a whirling devil that barks incessantly and in his frenzy, destroys everything in sight until you return. Many Boxers don't like to be left behind but will quickly settle down once the owner is gone and the dog is comfortable knowing that the

A "buddy" is one way to help alleviate your Boxer's boredom, and possibly even lessen his separation anxiety, but two dogs are literally twice the trouble and not the answer for most owners.

owner will be back. A dog that has true separation anxiety will have a frantic sound to his bark, may pace, drool, whine, scratch, or howl to the person who has left him behind.

If your Boxer has a problem about being left behind, there are several things you can do to help ease his worries.

- Help him bond to others. A dog that is overly dependent on one person is usually one that hasn't really bonded with anyone else. In other words, the owner is his sole reason for living. You can broaden your dog's social world by introducing other people for him to play with, perhaps even someone who can take him for a walk or play ball with him.
- Distract him. Give him something fun to do while you're gone. A good stuffable rubber toy filled with treats may be just the thing to ease his separation anxiety.
- Vary your routine. Sometimes owners are so routine that they actually cue their dogs that they are leaving. For instance, an owner may rattle her keys when she's on the way out the door, or perhaps, throw on a coat, or pick up a laptop by the door. If there are any departure cues you might be giving your dog, try to desensitize him to these cues by performing them on and off at times when you're *not* leaving.

When you do leave, do so quietly, and, if possible, vary the length of time you are gone. If you typically leave only for work and then are gone all day, try leaving for short trips, even if it's just in and out of the door.

- Keep your emotions in check. Making a big deal out of your dog's desire to be with you can fuel his separation anxiety rather than help alleviate it. If you coddle your dog when he begins his frantic barking, you are inadvertently reinforcing this behavior. Be sure to leave and return calmly and pet your dog only when he is behaving calmly.
- Introduce your Boxer to a crate. For serious cases of separation anxiety, a crate can be a very safe place. The dog has less chance of hurting himself in a crate, and cannot damage anything in your home. Be sure to condition him to his crate before you try to use it when you leave him (see Crate Training, page 26).
- Consult your veterinarian. In very serious cases of separation anxiety, a Boxer may lick himself raw or struggle so hard to escape his crate that he may seriously injure himself. In this instance, your veterinarian may recommend a conventional or holistic treatment to help calm your dog while you are working on behavioral changes.

13 *Noncompetitive Activities*

The Boxer is a working breed, which means she lives to work for you. If you'd like to take a step beyond training your dog for good manners and a few tricks, there are many activities in which you can become involved with your Boxer.

This chapter covers the noncompetitive activities in which Boxers excel, along with some ideas on getting started in these activities and some beginning training tips. For those who enjoy the thrill of competing, the following chapter covers several events in which you may be interested in training your dog to compete both with Boxers and other breeds or mixes of breeds.

For additional information and listings of related organizations on any or all of the activities listed in this chapter and Chapter 14, consult the Useful Addresses and Literature section at the end of this book.

Animal-assisted Therapy (AAT)

For years studies have indicated that human interaction with pets improves a person's quality of life, including the pet owner's mental and physical health.

That's why visiting pet programs are now recognized by many health care facilities to be an integral part of a patient's care plan.

Animal-assisted therapy (AAT) is a facet of health care that involve a visits and interaction with a pet. In some settings, AAT is treated with as much importance as any other therapy, such as physical, occupational, and speech therapies. The visits are structured and planned according to the individual patient's needs and are supervised by the health care facility. A less structured form of AAT is called "pet visitation," in which the visit from the pet is treated as more of a social event.

AAT is utilized in a variety of settings, including rehabilitation hospitals, pediatric acute care facilities, long-term nursing care, schools for the disabled, senior shut-ins, at-risk children's programs, hospices, mental health facilities, abuse shelters, orphanages, and even correctional facilities.

Certification requirements for AAT and pet visitation vary according to the certifying organization; however, you most likely will be required to achieve a Canine Good Citizen (CGC) certificate (see CGC, page 115), complete a training class geared toward AAT, pass a special test, and complete a one-on-one interview with your dog at an AAT testing facility.

The AAT test typically involves the dog's acceptance of a variety of situations she might encounter in a working therapy situation, such as a rolling wheelchair, a dropped pan, loud or sudden shouting, and uncontrolled movement. The potential therapy dog will also be tested on her reactions to some uncomfortable situations, such as a toe that is stepped on, a pulled ear, or a tug on her skin. Some certifying organizations may require that you and your Boxer take an aptitude test to evaluate what type of setting you are best suited for.

Many organizations, such as obedience clubs, kennel clubs, shelters, humane societies, and local AAT organizations, offer testing and certification for therapy work with a national organization. Recertification is generally required every couple of years, depending on the certifying organization. It is essential for liability reasons that you and your Boxer receive this certification if you wish to pursue this kind of work.

The outgoing yet gentle Boxer can make a wonderful therapy dog in a variety of settings.

Getting Started: AAT

1. **Reinforce Your Boxer's Commands.** Work with your Boxer until she is steady in the basic commands: sit, stay, stand, and come. She should also walk nicely on a leash.
2. **Socialize, Socialize, Socialize!** Introduce your Boxer as described in Chapter 5: Socialization. Try to have her meet as many different types of people as possible in a positive way.
3. **Go Everywhere with Her.** The more places you can take her, the more confident your Boxer will be in strange or unusual surroundings. That means take her on walks, up and down flights of steps, into buildings that accept dogs, such as your veterinarian's office. As she gains confidence, take her to more crowded areas, such as a sidewalk in town during the day. Practice walking on slick surfaces that you are likely to find in institutions.
4. **Groom Her and Bathe Her Regularly.** She will need to be immaculate for her therapy visits, which means you must minimize shedding and keep her tick and flea free. Her nails must also be kept short and smooth to prevent any chance of scratching a patient.

5. Enroll in a Class to Train for a Canine Good Citizen Certificate.
6. Locate a Club That Sponsors Testing for Certification with National AAT Therapy.

What It Takes for AAT

Does your Boxer have what it takes to become a therapy dog? Here's a brief checklist of qualities to look for.

- Gentleness
- A calm approach to most situations
- Not easily startled (curious is O.K.)
- Steady in basic commands
- Tolerant
- Well-socialized with all sort of people
- Enjoys physical praise

The backpack should be comfortable and fitted properly before you begin practicing carrying small loads with your dog.

Backpacking

If you enjoy camping or taking day hikes, you'll want to take your Boxer along. But why carry your supplies and your dog's when she can carry her supplies in a dog backpack? A dog in good shape and with no orthopedic problems should eventually be able to carry (with conditioning) up to one third of her weight in a properly fitted backpack.

Getting Started: Backpacking

1. **Get a Vet Check.** Most activities begin with a trip to the veterinarian; however, with backpacking it is essential that your Boxer is screened for any health problems that may make backpacking more difficult for her or even fatal. Your Boxer should be screened for hip dysplasia and heart problems.
2. **Have Control.** In order to backpack comfortably, your Boxer will need to be fairly obedient. In particular, you must be confident that she won't run off after a deer or a squirrel and knock you down (you'll be attached to her leash).
3. **Condition Your Boxer.** Just as people need to build up to hard exercise, Boxers will need to be conditioned for a day of hiking. Build up gradually and never push her beyond her limits. Always be wary of overheating her; brachycephalic dogs don't handle heat well.
4. **Choose a Comfortable Dog Backpack.** Ask someone who is experienced in

fitting backpacks to help you choose a backpack that fits your Boxer well. A pack that is padded is highly recommended since Boxers are shorthaired and don't have a thick coat to help cushion the straps. The backpack should be fitted so that the weight of the backpack will be near her shoulders and not on her back.

5. **Acclimate Her to the Backpack.** Begin by filling the backpack with towels (these are bulky but light) while taking her on her walks. When she is accustomed to this load, begin adding items that she will be carrying, such as her dog food, being careful to keep the backpack's load even.

6. **Check the Weather.** When you have finally built up to go hiking, make sure the weather is not too hot for your dog, and take a short hike at first.

7. **Check the Size of the Pack.** Be aware that your Boxer won't realize (initially) that the added width of the pack will catch on branches and undergrowth. Try to help her take it slowly until she learns the limits of her pack.

8. **Know First Aid.** Carry a first aid kit and know canine first aid (see Useful Addresses and Literature, page 134 for first aid book suggestions). A lot of unexpected things can happen when you are hours from help. Know what to do if your Boxer is injured and be sure to take preventive measures against fleas and ticks.

9. **Follow Trail Rules.** This means clean up after your dog, and always keep her on leash. The leash buckle can

attach to the backpack itself, or to her collar. The other end of the leash should be attached to your belt.

10. **Use identification.** Always use identification tags on your Boxer's collar, and clearly mark her backpack with your name and phone number.

What It Takes for Backpacking

■ Good general health
■ No hip or other joint problems
■ Endurance/conditioning
■ Good leash manners
■ Practice carrying a backpack

Canine Good Citizen

This certification was designed by the American Kennel Club (AKC) with the pet owner in mind. The Canine Good Citizen (CGC) test is sponsored by the AKC and tests the basic good manners of a dog, as well as emphasizing responsible pet ownership. The test is pass/fail and is noncompetitive. Dogs that pass the CGC receive certification from the AKC, as well as having their names recorded in the AKC's CGC archive. Owners may also elect to purchase CGC collar tags from the AKC that verify that dogs have passed the CGC test.

As previously mentioned, the CGC title is required by some AAT organizations for certification as a therapy. Additionally, 14 states have Canine Good Citizen resolutions to advance responsible dog

115

The Canine Good Citizen test requires that you and your Boxer can walk through a group of people without any signs of fearfulness or aggression by your dog.

Getting Started: Canine Good Citizen

The following are the ten items that your dog will be tested on for the CGC test. Remember. Your Boxer must pass *all* ten tests within the CGC to be certified. If you fail one, you will need to wait and practice for at least six months before you can be retested.

Test 1: Accepting a Friendly Stranger. In this test, you and your Boxer will approach a friendly stranger (usually the test evaluator) to shake hands and chat a little. Your Boxer must not show signs of aggression or fear, and must stay by your side.

Test 2: Sitting Politely for Petting. The second exercise of the CGC requires the friendly stranger to be able to touch your Boxer while she is sitting at your side. The evaluator will stroke your dog on her head and side, then walk around both you and her. She must be in control and must show neither fearfulness or aggression.

Test 3: Appearance and Grooming. In this exercise, the evaluator inspects the dog as a veterinarian or a judge might, including brushing her and examining her ears and both front paws.

Test 4: Out for a Walk (Walk on a Loose Leash). The fourth test checks to see if your Boxer will stay with you through a couple of stops, a left turn, right turn, and an about turn. Your Boxer doesn't need to be in perfect *heel* position, in fact, she can be on your left or right, slightly ahead or a little behind you. She is also not required to sit when you stop walking.

ownership. In the future, the CGC title may be one way to ensure homeowner's insurance coverage as more breeds are added to the "uncoverable" list.

Many training schools, 4-H centers, shelters, and even veterinary hospitals offer both training and testing for the CGC. The only requirements for participation in the training and testing programs are that your dog is up to date on her vaccinations. (She doesn't need to be an AKC-registered Boxer; paperless Boxers are welcome!)

Test 5: Walking through a Crowd. This test ensures that your Boxer will successfully navigate a crowd of people. You will be asked to walk and weave your way through a group of people. You may talk to her and encourage her throughout the exercise.

Test 6: Sit and Down on Command/Staying in Place. This tests your Boxer's ability to recognize and perform the *sit* and *down* commands, as well as a *sit-stay* or *down-stay.* On the *stay,* you will walk 20 feet (6 m) away from her. She must stay in place, but she can change positions (move from a sitting position to lying down or vice versa).

Test 7: Coming When Called. For this, your Boxer must prove she can stay on a *sit-stay* while you walk a distance of 10 feet (3 m) away from her, and then turn to face her. Then the evaluator will provide mild distractions, perhaps talking, walking past her, or petting her. She must stay in her position. Finally, you will be asked to call her, and she must come to you.

Test 8: Reaction to Another Dog. In this exercise, you will be required to approach another handler and dog team, stop, shake hands, chat, and then continue on your way, with your Boxer showing only mild curiosity in the other dog.

Test 9: Reactions to Distractions. In this exercise, the evaluator tests your dog's reactions to such sudden noises or events as a large book or pan being dropped, an umbrella being opened, or a runner jogging by. The evaluator looks to see if your dog responds negatively—fearfully or aggressively—to any of these or other situations.

Test 10: Supervised Separation. The final exam is designed to show your dog's ability to allow someone else to hold her leash briefly (three minutes) while you walk away from her. She doesn't have to maintain a *stay,* but she mustn't go berserk when you leave her with someone else.

What It Takes for CGC

- Any Boxer with basic training skills should be able to polish them up enough to achieve the CGC certification.
- Proof of up-to-date vaccinations are needed.
- Good socialization and habituation skills are needed.
- From four months old to 12 years, any age Boxer can test for this certification.

Disk Catching

Whether you someday compete in this sport, or simply teach your Boxer how to catch disks in the park, this activity is a fun one, and not too difficult to teach to her.

Getting Started: Disk Catching

1. **Get Your Boxer Interested in the Disk.** This usually isn't too hard, since most Boxers are up for any form of play—and if it involves a toy, well, they are there! If you have a puppy that is less certain of this plastic thing, get down

on the ground, roll the disk around a little, and shake it.

2. **Use the Take It Command (see Take It, page 79).** With the disk in your hand and directly in front of your Boxer's nose, give her the *take it* command. Praise her when she grabs it, and reward her by letting her run around a little with her prize.

3. **Keep a Line On.** To prevent your Boxer from getting into a major "chase me" game, be sure to attach a long recall leash, or even a tracking line (roughly 30-feet [9-m] long) on her.

Build up to the dog grabbing the disk in your hand while you give the *take it* command.

4. **Jump for It.** As your Boxer gets the hang of the *take it* command with the disk, begin moving it farther away from her (only a few feet) and have her jump forward—not up, yet—for it.

5. **Add a Swing.** If she's following along with you to this point, begin adding an arm swing with the *take it* command, and pause right before you'd normally let go of the disk to allow her to jump out and up to grab the disk.

6. **Toss It.** Now you're ready to add a slight toss to the disk. If your Boxer is hesitating, try tossing it to her. Be quick, though, because her reward is the disk. If she doesn't catch it, she doesn't get to play with it.

7. **Bring it Back!** Once you've got your Boxer chasing disks, your final step is to add the *recall.* With your line still attached, make short throws to her and ask her to *come* after she's caught the disk. If she's not steady on her *recall* yet, work on this exercise without the disk.

8. **Find a Disk That She Likes.** Disks come in soft and hard plastics, and even collapsible fabric models. Be careful never to let her chew them.

What It Takes for Disk Catching

- Enthusiasm and energy
- Good general health
- No hip or joint problems
- A strong drive for toys and, in particular, disks
- An owner who knows (or is willing to learn) how to throw a disk

118

Search and Rescue

Search and Rescue (SAR) teams are primarily volunteer organizations. (In some areas of the country, fire departments have SAR teams.) This means that handlers and their dogs respond to search for lost people or bodies, generally in areas that are difficult to search with just humans, such as forests, woods, and swamps. SAR teams are also called up to search disaster situations, such as the aftermaths of hurricanes, tornadoes, and explosions.

In very simplistic terms, the SAR dog may either be trained to "track," in which the dog finds and follows the actual foot path of the individual, or to "air scent," in which the dog is trained to scent for *any* human or a body and follows in the direction of the scent. SAR dogs may be taught to work closely with their handler, or to run ahead, find the victim, retrace their path, alert the handler to the find, and then return the handler to the victim. (Boxers during World War I in Germany performed this same function as medic dogs. As mentioned previously in this book, one Boxer was so good at finding wounded soldiers, retracing her steps, and leading medics to the soldiers that she was awarded the Iron Cross.)

Training for SAR requires a group effort: handlers, their dogs, and skilled trainers, who are often handlers, too, along with a corps of volunteers willing to trudge into the woods and wait for the handlers and dogs to find them. SAR handlers must also learn orienteering and survival techniques and pass a series of certifying tests with their dogs before they can work as an SAR team.

Participating in SAR (Search and Rescue) takes a lot of hard work by both owner and dog; however, the rewards of finding someone alive and returning him or her to safety is an untold satisfaction.

Getting Started: Search and Rescue

1. **Find a SAR Club.** One of the most important steps you'll need to take when considering training your Boxer for SAR work is to find a local or area club. Meet with members, talk to them about their dogs, how they train, how often they train, and what is expected of members.

2. **Train with a Mission.** To be a certified SAR team, you will be required to train for and pass a series of tests. Your local club will provide weekly—sometimes even twice a week or more—training sessions and will be able to guide you to the place you must travel to in order to be tested.

3. **Start Young.** If you have a puppy that is fully vaccinated, you can begin scent training with the SAR club. Many trainers feel that the younger the dog is started in this work, the more focused she is on scenting.

4. **Follow, Follow.** If you have a very young puppy, Norbert Zawatzki, director of training for the German Boxer Club, suggests beginning with a "cookie" trail. "Leave a short trail of little bits of dog cookies in a straight line," he recommends, "and begin your puppy with the first cookie." Encourage your puppy to follow the trail. Her reward, of course, is the cookies. Increase the distance in the trail, widening the gap between cookies.

5. Eventually, you can add a corner to your cookie trail and go longer distances. As your puppy progresses in tracking the cookies, you will progress to dragging the cookies a short distance to begin a trail.

What It Takes for SAR

Can the Boxer you own right now make a good SAR dog? It is possible. By nature, this breed possesses a high drive to work. Boxers also have a tremendous sense of smell. These two factors coupled with the Boxer's capacity for learning makes many Boxers potential SAR training candidates. The following is what is needed.

- A healthy, strong dog
- An equally healthy and strong owner
- A dog with lots of energy
- A strong drive to play with toys, which are often used as the rewards
- Good working obedience, though perfection is not necessary
- A dog that is well-socialized with people so that she won't growl, bite, or otherwise attack the "victim" once he or she is found
- An owner who has time to train on weekends and during the week
- An owner with a flexible schedule who is able to be on call 24 hours a day and take off on a moment's notice for a local, regional, or even international search or rescue

Swimming

Swimming is a fun activity for both Boxer and owner. Many of us live near a body of water (pond, lake, river, or ocean) or even have a pool in our backyards. The Boxer, as a deep-chested breed, is not naturally suited for swimming, so whether you are interested in taking her with you to the beach or in your pool, there are some precautions you should take.

Getting Started: Swimming

1. **Invest in a Properly-Fitted Canine Life Jacket.** This will help your Boxer, a dog that is not naturally very buoyant or an awesome swimmer, to feel more secure in the water. It will also give you something to grab if you need to pull her out.
2. **Keep It Quiet.** If you are taking your Boxer to the beach, make sure you take her when the ocean is very calm. Booming waves and heavy surf cannot only frighten a dog, but they can also be very dangerous.
3. **Start Young.** The sooner your Boxer is introduced to water, the more likely she will be accepting of this activity. When she's older and arthritic, she'll thank you for this wonderful form of exercise and therapy!
4. **Make a Slow Water Entry.** Whether you're introducing your Boxer to a pool, lake, or ocean, make the first steps small. In the pool, encourage her to step onto the first step with you. Praise her. Step farther into the pool and see if you can entice her farther in with a special toy. When she enters the water, hold her collar gently and grasp her under her chest to help her balance and float next to you. (Watch out for toenails!) Praise her when she starts paddling under water.
5. **Have Patience.** It may take up to eight sessions in the pool before your Boxer begins to figure out that this is really fun. You'll see her progress with every swim though.
6. **Teach the Exit.** Many dogs drown because they fall into pools and can't find the way out. Mark the steps with a

Take your dog out slowly the first several times in the pool and make sure she is wearing a life jacket to help her buoyancy.

visible marker, such as a red flag, and make sure to teach your Boxer where the steps are and exit with her each time this way.
7. **Lock the Gate.** Just as with children of any age, swimming should never be an unsupervised activity. Make sure your Boxer has access to the pool only when you can watch and when she has her life jacket on.

Training tips: Tracy Hendrickson, Founder, American Boxer Rescue Association; owner/trainer: Performance Boxer of the Year/2000.

What It Takes for Swimming

Any Boxer should be able to swim if she is introduced slowly to the activity with lots of positive reinforcement, and a life jacket.

14 *Competitive Activities*

If you enjoy the thrill of working as a team with your Boxer, and don't mind the heat of competition, or perhaps even thrive upon this kind of challenge, you'll be happy to know that there are many activities in which you and your Boxer might be well suited.

The following gives an introduction to six popular sports, some tips on getting started, and a checklist of attributes to see if your Boxer might be suited for a particular sport. Additional resources, including sanctioning organizations and further reading, are included in the Useful Addresses and Literature section of this book.

Agility

Agility is considered to be the fastest-growing dog sport in the United States. It is exciting to watch as a spectator, and even more exciting to participate in as a handler. Agility, in basic terms, is a competition that tests the dog and handler team's ability to negotiate a series of obstacles as fast as possible. The obstacles include tunnels, jumps, weave poles, see-saws, and suspended tires.

The handler's job is to direct the dog using only voice and hand signals through the course. The dog's job is to follow his master's directions as quickly as possible while running off lead. Most dogs, even those that are a bit shy, thoroughly enjoy this sport.

Many handlers begin Agility classes because they are looking for a fun outlet with their dogs, only to be so caught up in their dogs' enthusiasm for the sport that they decide to enter the competitive scene.

There are currently three major sanctioning organizations in the United States for Agility: the American Kennel Club (AKC), the North American Dog Agility Council (NADAC), and the United States Dog Agility Association (USDAA). Titles are awarded by each organization, and the requirements for each vary.

As for entries, NADAC and USDAA allow purebreds (registered and unregistered) and mixed-breeds to compete; however, the AKC allows purebreds *only*, and requires that participating dogs are AKC-registered or have an Indefinite Listing Privilege (ILP) number. ILP numbers are granted to Boxers that are judged (through photographs) to be purebred but are lacking registration papers.

Additionally, dogs competing in AKC Agility events must be at least a year old to enter; however, you might consider waiting until your Boxer is two years old to make sure that he is fully developed, free of hip disease, and perhaps less susceptible to injury.

Getting Started: Agility

1. **Get Grounded.** While you're waiting for your Boxer to be old enough to begin learning the various obstacles involved in the Agility events, take time to teach him to respond *well* to your verbal commands or hand signals. A very obedient dog will have a lot of fun with Agility!

2. **Clear Your Dog.** Make sure your Boxer is free of any hip or other musculoskeletal problems and is in good health. Agility is great fun and provides a good source of exercise, but if he has physical problems, some of the obstacles may exacerbate his condition.

3. **Socialize and Habituate Your Dog.** A confident dog will learn the obstacles of agility more readily than one that is fearful.

4. **Join an Agility Club.** If you have an enormous yard, time to spare, and money to spend, you could attempt to construct all the equipment used in Agility competitions. Then again, you could choose instead to join an Agility club, take training classes to introduce all the Agility obstacles, practice with other fun members, and use the club's facilities whenever you want. (You can still build a few of the smaller obstacles for backyard practices.)

5. **Never Rush.** Take your time with your Boxer and above all, keep it fun!

Agility requires very solid obedience and sound health.

What It Takes for Agility

- A healthy dog free of orthopedic problems that is at least 18 months old, preferably 24 months, or older
- Solid obedience skills of *down, come,* and *stay,* and the ability to work off leash
- Speed and agility (for competition)
- An owner who is in relatively good shape or who wants to get or keep in shape

Conformation

This is the only competitive event in which looks count. When you enter a Boxer in the conformation ring, a judge will closely examine the way your dog looks and moves and then compare him to the standard for the breed. The breed standard is a detailed description written and approved by the American Boxer Club that spells out what a perfect Boxer should look like from head to toe. If, in the opinion of the judge, your Boxer matches the breed standard more closely than the other dogs in the ring, the judge will "put up" or name your dog the winner of his class.

This is in theory, of course. Just as all owners think their Boxer is beautiful,

every judge has his or her own preferences within the breed and interprets the breed standard slightly differently. In other words, the world of judging and conformation is subjective.

Since the Boxer is also an extremely popular dog at the moment, competition is stiff, and in order to rack up the points needed to attain a championship, he will have to win over a lot of other good-looking Boxers. Showing in conformation requires a lot of time, money, and travel. Though it is more difficult for an amateur owner/handler to show and win with a dog (even when the dog is very good), it is *not* impossible (see below). A solid dog *will* finish; it just may take a little longer.

Owners who wish to "finish"a dog (attain a championship) but don't want to handle the dog themselves, can hire professional handlers. The handler provides the Boxer owner with two things: a polished, professional presentation of your Boxer to the judge, and the political edge of having a known handler—who only accepts good dogs to present, of course—bringing your dog into the ring.

For conformation events, you will need to learn how to stack your dog for the show ring as well as how to gait your dog in the ring.

Getting Started: Conformation

1. **Learn the Ropes.** Go to shows and watch carefully how the professionals handle their dogs. Learn and understand the point system, as well as the different classes in which you can enter. Talk to other Boxer breeders and owners, listen, and learn.
2. **Evaluate Your Boxer Honestly.** Before you take the plunge to begin training

your Boxer for the conformation ring, ask your breeder if he or she feels your dog is capable of attaining a championship. If your breeder is, for some reason, not available to help you, you may be able to find another reputable breeder willing to help you evaluate your Boxer.

3. **Learn and Practice "Stacking."** If your puppy is going to make his entrance in the show, he'll have to know how to stand still and keep his feet where you place them. There are dogs that literally can't put a foot down wrong, but most dogs can and do put their feet down in awkward positions which can amplify or bring attention to a fault. Use the *stand-stay* command to keep your Boxer in position, and get him used to you moving his feet into place.

4. **Play Judge.** Have friends and neighbors practice checking your Boxer's teeth, eyes, ears, and body. He will need to stay immobile during this process, which means he can't get too excited or begin to jump around. He also cannot pull back or otherwise shy away from the judge. Any act of aggression will get you and your pet tossed from the ring. Be sure to practice the *stand for examination* with people who smell differently. There have been many stories of dogs that were not timid at all, but would shy away from hands smelling heavily of cigarette smoke or cologne.

5. **Go through the Paces.** When in the show ring, you will need to be able to "gait" your dog, or trot briskly around the ring to show off your dog's front, back, and side movement. Your Boxer will need to be able to move comfortably on a slender slip collar and lead used for showing—and not drag you around uncontrollably. He will also need to learn (and so will you) how to do an about-turn without changing sides (for instance, walk on your left away from the judge and about-turn so that you simply change lead hands and walk back with your Boxer on your right side). You'll also need to master the basic "L" patterns in the show ring.

6. **Take a Conformation Class.** The best way to learn the movements of the show ring and to polish your performance is by attending a conformation class with your Boxer. These are typically held by obedience clubs and are generally offered on a regular basis. Even if you plan on hiring a professional handler, your Boxer will need to know what to do in the ring.

7. **Go to Fun Matches.** These matches are for fun, literally. They are not official shows, but they can be used for training. You may also be able to get a better idea about whether your Boxer and you really do have what it takes to achieve a championship.

What It Takes for the Show Ring

- Conformation that is as close to the breed standard as possible with few if any faults.
- Good movement. It's not just good enough to "look" good, a potential champion must move well, too.

- Solid temperament. The Boxer that loves to perform in the show ring is generally, with all else being equal, the one no one can take their eyes off of.
- Professional presentation. You can have the most gorgeous Boxer in the world, but if you bumble the handling and *look* like an amateur in the ring, many judges won't consider your dog. Make sure that if you are handling your Boxer, you handle him professionally.
- Winners all. Remember that no matter how your dog does in the ring, he is *your* Boxer and that automatically counts for something in your heart. Treat him like the champion he is, whether or not he wears the title! "They are my beloved pets *first*. The rest is icing on the cake," notes Tracy Hendrickson, whose Sunchase Boxers have certainly won their share of conformation and performance titles!

Flyball

Flyball is a team sport that packs a lot of excitement into just a few minutes of competition. Flyball enjoys pockets of popularity in the United States, so it is not available everywhere yet. If you have the opportunity to train with a local flyball team, or if you're interested in forming your own team (think of the fun an all-Boxer team would have!), both you and your Boxer will enjoy yourselves.

Flyball involves relay teams of four dogs and handlers. The dogs, one at a time, race over a 51-foot (15-m) course with four hurdles. At the end of the straight course of hurdles is a box. The dog must run to the box, hit a lever with his foot, which hurls a tennis ball up in the air, catch the ball, and race back over the course of jumps to the start, where the next dog on the team now takes off.

The winner of each heat is determined by the fastest time weighted against any deductions for errors, such as dropping a ball or missing a jump. Two teams participate in each heat in a single-elimination flyball tournament. Hurdles are set 4-inches (10-cm) lower than the shoulder height of the smallest dog on each team, with a minimum hurdle height of 8 inches (20 cm) and a maximum of 16 inches (40 cm).

The sanctioning organization is the North American Flyball Association. Titles are awarded through this organization and are based on a point system. NAFA reports that there are more than 300 member clubs across the country, and more than 7,000 dogs registered in the sport.

Getting Started: Flyball

1. **Speed Up the Recall.** In flyball, there is a need for speed. One area in which many competitors find they need work is in the speed of the *recall.* Many a dog has been delighted to run to the flyball box knowing that he can pop out a ball, and then be less than enthusiastic to bring the ball back. To speed up your Boxer's *recall,* you can work on the *recall* exercises (see Come, page 69). You can also increase your dog's drive to come to you by having someone hold him while you call him with great excitement and the

prospect of a good treat, or a particularly favorite toy.

2. **Encourage the Ball Drive.** The more ball crazy your Boxer is, the faster he's going to run to the ball box. One way to increase his ball drive is to not let him play with balls except when you're working with him.

3. **Keep Things Healthy.** Make sure that before you begin participating in flyball, as with any sport, your Boxer is in good health and free of any conditions that might be aggravated by running hard and jumping hurdles.

What It Takes for Flyball

- No dog-dog aggression
- Enthusiasm and high energy
- A craze for balls
- Good health

Obedience

Competing in obedience trials can be done on two very different personal levels: You can work to attain obedience titles on your Boxer, or you can compete to win or place in your class or trial. Which level you decide to compete at is entirely up to you and your Boxer.

The first level is that of attaining titles. At this level, you have fun working with your Boxer, he has fun working with you, and you aren't as concerned with how high your score is as much as achieving the "legs" necessary to attain the title. At this level, the only pressure that is on you is the pressure you place on yourself.

If your Boxer is nuts over balls, he might do well in flyball.

At the higher level, you are training your Boxer to be as flawless as possible. Your goal is not merely to pass each judged test, but to score so highly that you are in a position to place in or win your class. You might even have your eye on a "High in Trial" trophy, or perhaps you might be working toward an obedience championship. Depending on your skills as a trainer and your Boxer's potential as an obedience whiz, these goals are not out of sight for you.

In fact, virtually every Boxer—with training of course—should be able to achieve his "Companion Dog" (CD) title. The CD is offered through AKC-sanctioned trials and is the entry level into the world of obedience. (The United Kennel Club also offers obedience trials and titles. See Useful Addresses and Literature for more

127

information.) If you've never entered a dog in an obedience trial before, you'll be able to enter Novice A. If you've trained a dog and tested at an AKC-sanctioned obedience trial, then you will need to enter Novice B. In order to earn a CD, your Boxer will need to receive passing scores at three different trials under three different judges. A passing score requires a minimum of 170 points out of 200 possible points.

The exercises for the CD title include: *heeling on lead* and *heeling in a figure 8* (40 points); off-lead *stand for examination* (30 points); *heeling off lead* (40 points); *recall* exercise (30 points); *sit-stay* for one minute (30 points); and *down-stay* for three minutes (30 points).

Getting Started: Obedience

1. **Find a Good Training Club.** You can train your Boxer by yourself using a myriad of books written for both the novice handler and the advanced superstar; however, it is difficult to replicate all the different training scenarios without help. Training clubs also are comprised of trainers and dog owners with a variety of experience, which, if they are willing to share their expertise freely with you, can provide you with a wealth of training tips and problem solving abilities.

2. **Perfect Practice Makes Perfect.** As authors Mary R. Burch, Ph.D. and Jon S. Bailey, Ph.D. so concisely sum up in *How Dogs Learn* (New York: Howell Books, 1999), "'Practice makes perfect' isn't exactly true. *Perfect* practice makes perfect." What this means is that the skilled trainer makes fewer training mistakes and therefore rarely has to backtrack or "undo" inadvertent training errors. When training under a skilled trainer for competitive obedience, you will make fewer mistakes as a trainer,

Each level of Obedience requires that your Boxer perform more difficult exercises, such as this *recall* over a bar jump.

and your Boxer will learn more quickly and with fewer roadblocks.

3. **Keep the Enthusiasm and Attention!** An enthusiastic Boxer performing obedience is an awesome sight.

4. **Take It Slowly.** Don't rush your Boxer. Take it at his speed. Be patient. Sometimes it will seem that you're not making any progress, then the light will shine. Persevere!

5. **Practice Early Heeling Exercises for Focus.** Some animal behaviorists estimate that if a puppy doesn't learn to focus on his master by the time he reaches four or five months old, you will be competing for his attention from then on. This means that your puppy really should be walking nicely on a leash (see Walk Nicely, page 72) and focusing on you by the time he is five months old.

6. **Introducing Dumbbells Early.** If you plan on gaining titles beyond the entry level CD, be sure you introduce dumbbell work to your puppy at an early age. Using a plastic dumbbell, practice the *take it* and *out* commands (see Take It and Out, page 79) from time to time. Don't allow your Boxer to play with the dumbbell unsupervised or allow him to chew on it. Rather, make taking and releasing the dumbbell a "special" fun game he can play only with you.

What It Takes for Obedience

■ A Boxer. Every Boxer should be able to successfully attain his CD title.

■ An enthusiastic, energetic Boxer that is capable of focusing.

■ Creative handling. Boxers bore easily and need an owner who can think of ways to keep learning a fun and new experience.

■ Patience. Boxers are not ready to focus quite as early as some other breeds, so owners must realize that this process can't be rushed—but to keep working at it!

Rally-style Obedience

This new sport is similar to obedience; however, the owner and dog team perform all the exercises in one continuous motion. Handlers are allowed to talk to their dogs, as well as praise and encourage them verbally. It's exciting, fast paced, and a lot of fun.

Current rules require a rally course to consist of 25 to 28 different exercises, depending on the level of competition. The competition is divided into two levels: Level 1, which is on leash and has a course that uses only 25 possible maneuvers; and Level 2, which is off leash and uses 25 to 28 of 44 possible maneuvers. Exercises include changes in pace, spirals to the left and right, jumps, about-turns, and figure 8s.

Three qualifying scores of 170 points out of a possible 200 under three different judges are required for a title. The AKC recently added rally-style obedience as a non-regular class. As more people are introduced to the sport, its support is expected to grow rapidly. For more

Rally-style Obedience was approved as a non-regular class in AKC Obedience trials in November 2000.

information, see Useful Addresses and Literature, page 134.

Schutzhund

Though perhaps mostly known for the protection segment of the test, Schutzhund is a sport that includes much more, including competitions and titles in endurance, obedience, tracking, and, Schutzhund itself, which is a three-part test of obedience, tracking, and protection work.

Schutzhund is *not* a means to train a protection dog; it is only a sport and should be taught using positive reinforcement and play training. Those who seek Schutzhund sport because they feel unsafe in their homes think that this training will provide protection; however, they'd be better off installing an alarm system in their homes. If the protection portion of Schutzhund is taught correctly, the Boxer will only bite the arm of a "bad guy" if he is wearing a special protective sleeve. This is because this sport is taught as a sport only, and uses play-based training. In order to get a Boxer to bite and hold onto the "helper's" arm in competition, the dog is taught to play tug with the padded sleeve. He has no intention of hurting the person wearing the sleeve. In fact, if you were to give a properly trained Schutzhund Boxer the command to "bite" someone who didn't have a sleeve on, he would be very confused. It would be very much like telling your Boxer to fetch a ball when you hadn't thrown anything.

So why does Schutzhund have such a bad reputation in the United States? Because serious problems can and do occur in protection work when owners don't use play training, and instead attempt to train using defensive methods in which the Boxer is truly taught to attack. There are some clubs in the United States that reportedly do train this way, so it is best to avoid any club that doesn't strictly use play training to teach this sport. Additionally, this is not a sport that can be idly dabbled with: To be successful, you must be dedicated to working with your Boxer regularly and training under a very experienced trainer.

With this said, if you are considering training your Boxer in any level of Schutzhund, you need to consider this: Schutzhund-trained dogs are discriminated against by some insurance agencies, as well as by some neighborhood associations. In other words, if you attain Schutzhund titles with your Boxer, you may find that your homeowner's policy is revoked, or even that you might not be able to continue living in your neighborhood! Before beginning training in this sport, it is important to investigate your local regulations as well as reading the fine print in your homeowner's policy.

Getting Started: Schutzhund

1. **Find a Play-based Training Club.** This point cannot be emphasized enough.
2. **Look for a Boxer-savvy Trainer.** German Shepherd Dogs and Belgian Malinois dominate this sport. Their training is very different from a Boxer's. (They are capable of focusing intensely at a much earlier age, for example, and are less likely to attempt to provide comic relief for their handlers.) If you can find someone who enjoys working with Boxers, you will be that much farther ahead in training.

Schutzhund is now taught using operant conditioning and positive reinforcement. Biting the protective sleeve of the helper is only a game for these dogs.

Schutzhund also involves Obedience and tracking.

3. Be Prepared to Commit a Great Deal of Time. This sport requires many facets of training, beginning with obedience training and tracking, and finally—if you choose to participate in this area—protection work.

What It Takes for Schutzhund

- Good health and a sound body. The obedience title with Schutzhund requires jumping a substantial fence and climbing a large A-frame, among other activities. Boxers should be cleared of any health or physical problems before participating in these events.
- No aggression. With protection work, the Boxer must be self-confident, possess a stable and sound temperament, and

not be aggressive. There is no place for aggression in this sport.
- No fearful or timid temperaments.

Tracking

Both the AKC and Schutzhund clubs sanction tracking tests, and Boxers do well at both. AKC tracking tests offer three levels, which are pass/fail and are noncompetitive, and a tracking championship. Schutzhund sport offers a tracking title, as well as competition.

The only disadvantage Boxers may have with tracking is that because they are a brachycephalic breed, they do not tolerate hot temperatures well and shouldn't be asked to work when the temperatures are too high. Depending on where you live, the climate may not be a problem, or may be a concern only during the peak summer months.

In tracking, the dog must not only follow the trail left by a person through various vegetation and terrain, but he must also indicate any articles left by the person along the trail. This involves a lot of time spent training with your dog, and requires the support of a good tracking club. (This sport is definitely a group effort!)

If your dog is particularly good at tracking and attains one or more tracking titles, you might consider sharing his talents by volunteering with a local SAR team (see Search and Rescue, page 119). This public service demands a lot of time and effort; however, locating a lost person and saving a life—or even finding a body and providing closure to a family—provide untold rewards for both you and your Boxer.

Getting Started: Tracking

1. **Begin Early.** Though an old Boxer can learn new tricks, many tracking instructors recommend working on your dog's scenting abilities at an early age. As soon as he is fully vaccinated, you can begin early tracking training.
2. **Get in Shape.** Tracking is not for the weak or physically frail owner. It involves moving swiftly through potentially rugged terrain.
3. **Find a Good Training Club.** As mentioned earlier, tracking is a group

effort and requires skilled training. Training with a tracking club will give you access to expert advice, as well as training grounds where tracks can be laid and a variety of skills worked on.

4. **Keep It Positive.** Your Boxer loves to work and tracking may be the perfect sport for him. To keep his enthusiasm and enjoyment up, be sure to keep your training positive and provide plenty of rewards.

What It Takes for Tracking

- Good health and fitness—both dog and handler
- Energy and enthusiasm
- Good scenting abilities

Boxers can compete in tracking through AKC tests and Schutzhund trials.

Useful Addresses and Literature

Organizations

American Boxer Club
Corresponding Secretary, Mrs. Barbara E.
    Wagner
6310 Edward Drive
Clinton, MD 20735-4135
Breeder Contact, Mrs. Lucille Jackson
11300 Oakton Road
Oakton, VA 22124
(703) 385-9385
Web site: *http://clubs.akc.org/abc/*
    abc-hom.htm

Note: Contact names change periodically.
Please confirm current contacts through
the ABC web site, or by calling the American Kennel Club.

American Boxer Rescue Association
    (ABRA)
Tracy Hendrickson
4412 W. Kent Circle
Broken Arrow, OK 74014
(918) 665-1765
Web site: *www.jps.net/Boxer4me*

United States Boxer Association
W3595 Larson Road
Mindoro, WI 54644
Web site: *http://members.aol.com/usabox*

Boxer-Klub E.V. Sitz München
Veldener Str 64+66, 81241 Munich,
    Germany
011 49-89-54670812
Web site: *www.bk-muenchen.de/english.*
    htm

American Kennel Club
5580 Centerview Drive, Suite 200
Raleigh, NC 27606-3390
(919) 233-3600
Web site: *www.akc.org*

United Kennel Club
100 E. Kilgore Road
Kalamazoo, MI 49001-5598
(616) 343-9020
Web site: *http://www.ukcdogs.com/*

Activities/Behavior

Agility
Agility Association of Canada (AAC)
RR #2
Lucan, ONT Canada NON 2J0
(519) 657-7636

North American Dog Agility Council
(NADAC)
HRC@, Box 277
St. Maries, ID 83861

United States Dog Agility Association
(USDAA)
P.O. Box 850955
Richardson, TX 75085
(214) 231-9700
Web site: www.usdaa.com

Animal-assisted Therapy
The Delta Society
289 Perimeter Road East
Renton, WA 98055-1329
(800) 869-6898
Web site: www.deltasociety.com

Therapy Dogs International, Inc.
88 Bartley Road
Flanders, NJ 07836
(973) 252-9800
Web site: www.tdi_dog.org

Behavior
Animal Behavior Society
2611 East 10th Street, Office 170
Indiana University
Bloomington, IN 47408-2603
(812) 856-5541
Web site: www.animalbehavior.org/ABS

American Veterinary Medical Association
1931 N. Meacham Road, Suite 100
Schaumburg, IL 60173-4360
(847) 925-8070

Canine Good Citizen
Canine Good Citizen Department
American Kennel Club
5580 Centerview Drive
Raleigh, NC 27606
(919) 852-3875
Web site: www.akc.org/love/cgc/index.cfm

Conformation
(See American Kennel Club listing.)
Web site:
http://www.akc.org/dic/events/conform/
index.cfm

Deaf Boxers
Deaf Dog Education Action Fund (DDEAF)
P.O. Box 369
Boonville, CA 95415
Web site: www.deafdogs.org
E-mail: Ddeaf@aol.com
Deaf Dog FAQ
Leslie Judkins, research chairperson of the
DDEAF
To receive a copy, e-mail: ljudkins@ix.
netcom.com
DDEAF Survey
Web site: http://www.deafdogs.org/
survey.html.

Deaf Dog Mailing List
E-mail: deaf-dogs-request@cybervision.
kwic.net
Type "subscribe deaf dogs" in the subject
of your e-mail and type your name and
e-mail address in the text of the e-mail.

Deaf Dogs Web Page
Web site:
http://www.kiva.net/~lindsay/deafdogs/

Deaf Dog Research

Author Susan Cope Becker is gathering information on deaf canine tempera-ments. If you own a deaf Boxer and would like to participate in the survey, you can get a copy of the question-naire from Becker's book, *Living with a Deaf Dog* (see below), or by contacting Becker at the following e-mail address: scope2000@aol.com

Deaf Dog/Vibrating Collar Sources

Vibratel

Web site: *http://pcola/gulf.net/~bbishop/ index.html*

E-mail: bbishop@pcola.gulf.net

Tri-Tronics

P.O. Box 17660

Tucson, AZ 85731

(520) 290-6000

Web site: *http://www.tritronics.com*

E-mail: infor@tritronics.com

Vibrating Collar Instructions (homemade)

Web site: *http://www.lsu.edu/guests/ senate/public_html/CollarInstructions. html.*

Disk Catching

International Disk Dog Handlers Association (IDDHA)

1690 Julius Bridge Road

Ball Ground, GA 30107

(770) 735-6200

Web site: *www.iddha.com/*

Flying Disk Dog Open

Bill Watters/Director

P.O. Box 4615

Cave Creek, AZ 85327

(888) 383-3357

(480) 595-0580 in Arizona

Web site: *www.airmajorsdoghouse.com/ fddo/*

The QUADRUPED

Jeff Hoot, Director

Hoot@TheQuadruped.com

Rt. 1 Box 445

Bryceville, FL 32009

(904) 266-4000

Web site: *www.TheQuadruped.com/ Toc.htm*

Flyball

North American Flyball Association (NAFA)

1400 Devon Avenue, Box 512

Chicago, IL 60660

Obedience

(See American Kennel Club listing.)

Web site: *www.akc.org/dic/events/ obedtrack/akcobed.cfm*

(See United Kennel Club listing.)

Web site: *www.ukcdogs.com/obedience. html*

Association of Pet Dog Trainers (APDT)

P.O. Box 385

Davis, CA 95617

(800) 738-3647

Web site: *www.apdt.com*

National Association of Dog Obedience Instructors (NADOI)

P.O. Box 432

Landing, NJ 07785

Rally-style Obedience
(See American Kennel Club information.)

Rally-style Obedience
c/o Charles L. Kramer
401 Bluemont Circle
Manhattan, KS 66502-4531
(785) 537-7022
E-mail: KramerC@ksu.edu

Rally-style Obedience mailing list
For membership, send a blank e-mail to:
    Rally-obed-subscribe@egroups.com

Schutzhund
DVG America
Secretary: Sandi Prudy
5718 Watson Circle
Dallas, TX 75225
Web site: *http://webusers.anet-stl.com/~dvgamer*

United Schutzhund Clubs of America
3810 Paule Avenue
St. Louis, MO 63125
(314) 638-9686
E-mail: usaschutzhund@worldnet.att.net
(See United States Boxer Association listing.)

Search and Rescue
American Rescue Dog Association
P.O. Box 151
Chester, NY 10918
Web site: *www.ardainc.org*

Tracking
(See American Kennel Club listing.)
Web site: *www.akc.org/dic/events/obedtrack/trackreg.cfm*
(See Schutzhund listing.)

Books

Activities
Agility: Simmons-Moake, Jane. *Agility Training, the Fun Sport for All Dogs.* New York: Howell Book House, 1992.

Animal-assisted Therapy: Burch, Mary R. and Aaron Honori Katcher. *Volunteering with Your Pet: How to Get Involved in Animal-Assisted Therapy with Any Kind of Pet.* New York: Howell Book House, 1996.

Davis, Kathy Diamond. *Therapy Dogs: Training Your Dog to Reach Others.* New York: Howell Book House, 1992.

Backpacking: LaBelle, Charlene. *A Guide to Backpacking with Your Dog.* Loveland, CO: Alpine Publications, 1992.

Canine Good Citizen: Volhard, Jack and Wendy Volhard. *The Canine Good Citizen: Every Dog Can Be One,* 2nd edition. New York: Howell Book House, 1997.

Conformation: Coile, Caroline D. *Show Me! A Dog Show Primer.* Hauppauge, NY: Barron's Educational Series, 1997.

Hall, Lynn. *Dog Showing for Beginners.* New York: Howell Book House, 1994.

Stern, Jane and Michael Stern. *Dog Eat Dog: A Very Human Book about Dogs and Dog Shows.* New York: Simon & Schuster Trade, 1998.

First Aid: Heath, Sebastian and Andrea O'Shea. *Rescuing Rover: A First Aid and Disaster Guide for Dog Owners.* West Lafayette, Indiana: Purdue University Press, 1999.

Flyball: Olson, Lonnie. *Flyball Racing: The Dog Sport for Everyone.* New York: Macmillan General Reference, 1997.

Obedience: Bauman, Diane. *Beyond Basic Dog Training.* New York: Howell Book House, 1991.

Handler, Barbara. *Successful Obedience Handling: The New Best Foot Forward.* Loveland, CO: Alpine Publications, Inc., 1991.

Schutzhund: Barwig, Susan. *Schutzhund: Theory and Training Methods.* New York: Howell Book House, 1991.

Search and Rescue: American Dog Rescue Association. *Search and Rescue Dogs: Training Methods.* New York: Howell Book House, 1991.

Tracking: Brown, Tom. *The Science and Art of Tracking.* New York: Penguin USA, 1999.

Sanders, William. *Enthusiastic Tracking: The Step-by-Step Training Handbook.* Stanwood, WA: Rime Publications, 1998.

Behavior/Training

General Behavior: Burch, Mary R. and Jon S. Bailey. *How Dogs Learn.* New York: Howell Book House, 1999.

Coren, Stanley. *How to Speak Dog: Mastering the Art of Dog-Human Communication.* New York: The Free Press, 2000.

Fogle, Bruce. *The Dog's Mind: Understanding Your Dog's Behavior.* New York: Howell Book House, 1990.

Behaviors (Problem): Houpt, Katherine A. and Myrna Watanabe, editors. *Dealing with Your Dog's Aggressive Behavior.* Stratford, CT: Torstar Publications, Inc., 1999.

Ryan, Terry. *The Toolbox for Remodeling Your Problem Dog.* New York: Howell Book House, 1998.

Weston, David and Ruth Weston. *Dog Problems: The Gentle Modern Cure.* New York: Howell Book House, 1992.

Clicker Training: Pryor, Karen. *Getting Started: Clicker Training for Dogs.* Waltham, MA: Sunshine Books, Inc., 1999.

Spector, Morgan. *Clicker Training for Obedience.* Waltham, MA: Sunshine Books, Inc., 1999.

Deaf Dog Training: Becker, Susan Cope. *Living With a Deaf Dog,* 2nd edition. Cincinnati, Ohio: Susan Cope Becker, 1998.

Eaton, Barry. *Hear, Hear! A Guide to Training a Deaf Puppy,* 2nd edition. Hampshire, England: Holmes & Sons, 1998.

Sternberg, Martin L.A. *American Sign Language Dictionary.* New York, Harper Reference, 1998.

General Training: Dunbar, Ian. *How to Teach a New Dog Old Tricks,* 2nd edition. Oakland, CA: James and Kenneth Publishers, 1991.

Pryor, Karen. *Don't Shoot the Dog.* Waltham, MA: Sunshine Books, 1984.

Head Halter Training: Fields-Babineau, Miriam. *Dog Training with a Head Halter.* Hauppauge, NY: Barron's Educational Series, 2000.

House-training: Kalstone, Shirlee. *How to Housebreak Your Dog in 7 Days.* New York: Bantam Books, 1985.

Index